IDEAS THAT COULD CHANGE YOUR LIFE

LIFE LESSONS
FROM A SERIAL
ENTREPRENEUR

CARL WOLF

Life Lessons from a Serial Entrepreneur:
Ideas that Could Change Your Life

ISBN Paperback: 979-8-89576-142-7

Published by:

For my wife, Marion, who is my love, my life, and business partner. She was the rock who kept Alpine Lace and our food brokerage business together, and advised me all along the way. Thank you always.

Also for my son-in-law and business partner, Matt Brown. We had an excellent and productive business relationship for twenty-three years, founded on mutual respect.

And also, for my dear daughter, Karen, a brilliant designer and marketer, who applied her considerable skills to our appetizer product, moving the brand into an online presence with 300,000 visitors a month. She also shared in the family business decisions.

Matt, Karen, and Marion were my three key business advisors who made a big difference in the success I enjoyed.

Table of Contents

Introduction

If I could sum up in one sentence what I want you to get from reading this book, I'd say that I want you to have "aha!" moments.

Maybe they'll come because you read one of my stories and caught a glimpse of wisdom or a lesson you had never considered. Better yet, I hope one or more of my stories jogs your memory, and your "aha!" will be, "I knew that, and now I remember that I knew that!" Best case scenario? You'll internalize one or two or more lessons and take them with you into the world. I hope they have an impact. I want them to make your life better.

I don't plan to bore you with the long, drawn-out story of my life as a serial entrepreneur, but I will tell you the stories that matter: the ones that changed me, the ones I learned from, the ones I failed to learn from, and the ones that propelled me to success. Think of this as a business book with stories and lessons embedded in it.

I was young when I internalized my first lessons. What we learn in those early years sets the stage for the values we hold throughout our lives, whether we learn from observing others or through what we are told directly by our parents or other influential adults. Sometimes the most impactful lessons show us what not to do.

My father was an egg wholesaler to supermarkets and restaurants. He would often add smaller eggs to cartons marked "large." I knew it was wrong, and I swore I would never do that.

I promised myself I would be an honest person.

Honesty has always been my pole star.

A couple of years ago, I was talking with my friend, Ross Lewis, telling him some of my stories, probably including the one about the eggs. "You know," he said, "you should write a book."

I thought about that for a minute. "A book about my business?"

"No. A book about what you learned."

Hmmm. Maybe. And then I wondered who would read it. As I thought about the idea, I began to recall the stories of my life and the lessons I had learned, from the failures of an Olympics-branded cheese to a wildly successful Italian food company. I realized I had anecdotes worth telling, both for entertainment value and for lessons learned.

I hope this book entertains you.

I hope it gives you "aha!" moments.

I hope that when you put it down, you'll be better equipped to live your life boldly and successfully.

I learned as much or more from my failures than I did from my successes. I have no agenda. There isn't one single tenet for this book. I'm not going to tell you what you should glean from these pages, and I won't tell you that the secret to success is dressing professionally, being able to speak well in public, or breaking your people into different kinds of teams. I don't think there is one single answer to success. What works for you may not work for your neighbor.

I can tell you my stories, and hopefully, you'll see something in them that you can take into your own life; something that will help you discover your own magic formula.

I was talking with a friend recently about John Krakauer's book, *Into Thin Air*, the true story of a 24-hour period on Everest, when members of three separate expeditions were caught in a storm and faced a battle against hurricane-force winds, exposure, and the effects of altitude, which ended in the worst single-season death toll in the peak's history.

The book stuck with me because it hinged on a series of small mistakes, one on top of another. The book is a lesson about making compromises. I've made those too in my career. My tragedies certainly never equaled those on Everest, but I learned that compromises can easily lead to failure.

One lesson I learned early in my career is that entrepreneurs make mistakes. Probably 70% of every new thing they try is a misstep. But successful entrepreneurs clean up those mistakes and move on.

I hope my book encourages you to go on your journey of discovery. I'm not extraordinary. We all have led remarkable lives full of astonishing stories. I believe it was Oprah who once said, "Everybody has a story. And there's something to be learned from every experience."

I'm telling mine. Or at least parts of mine. Perhaps this book will help you tell yours. You'll be richer for remembering it. I want to invite you on this journey with me, in the hopes it will remind you of your own.

And if you are still near the beginning of your career and life trek, I hope the lessons I offer will help you make good choices. Life lessons are what you make of them.

CHAPTER 1

Lessons of Youth

I wasn't born privileged or wealthy. My father was an egg wholesaler and distributor, selling to restaurants and supermarkets. My first job in high school was candling eggs, which involved placing eggs under a light source to eliminate the ones with blood spots and cracks, and placing them in cartons. My second job, starting in my senior year of high school and right into college, was as a shoe salesman.

I was always confident and assertive. My father was domineering, easily imposing his will on my brothers and sister. I was the only one who stood up to him, and as a result, I think he respected me.

What made me different? What made me declare my autonomy? Perhaps it was simply my nature. But I was the shining star of my family, and I'm sure that had a strong influence on my confidence and assertiveness.

When I was very young, I had polio, and in third grade, I told my teacher, Mrs. Johnson, that I'd had polio.

She said, "There's no way you had polio."

She doubted me? I walked home that day and insisted my mother write a note telling my teacher the facts.

I don't remember the details, but I suspect I placed that note on her desk the next day with a certain "so there!" flourish.

I was a good student and had a lot of friends. Many of my older brother's friends were also mine, probably because I was confident beyond my years.

We grew up in the 1950s in a fairly typical middle-class neighborhood. I don't recall ever feeling deprived, but we certainly weren't rich. Every year, we'd vacation at a beach town for several weeks, and I remember loving our summers there.

By the time I entered Rutgers University in 1961, I was basically paying my own way with the help of two scholarships. I wanted independence and was proud of it. I didn't want to owe anything to my family.

I remember my mother with some fondness, although she became bitter as the years passed. Perhaps she expected too much and took offense where none was intended. She wasn't comfortable in social situations outside the family, but she would spend hours on the phone with her mother or sister, or my great-aunt Ruth.

My grandmother tended to be self-absorbed, but my wife and I both adored her. She lived every minute of her life to the fullest. She spent her life in pursuit of money, and she was always short. Her first husband died of a heart attack. She then married a man she thought was rich. It turned out he wasn't. When he died, she married her third husband, who she also believed was wealthy. He also had no vast sums of money. Still, she had enough, but she wanted more.

She would take the bus to Klein's Discount Department Store in downtown Newark to browse the sale rack twice a week, keeping an eye on the clothes she liked and watching for further markdowns. When the price was low enough, she'd buy the dress or blouse or jacket.

Every day, she would sit in the gallery of her local stockbroker's office. She had very little money to risk, but she'd watch the ticker tape.

Eventually, she lost what little she had, but by that time, I had graduated and slipped some money to the stockbroker to soften the blow.

My childhood had its challenges, but I grew up in a good time and place. We lived in Newark, where our gang of kids was always busy playing stickball, football, or basketball, or we'd sit out on the porch telling stories. Summers were glorious. No one had air conditioning, so we'd be outside calling back and forth to our neighbors or playing on the sidewalk in front of the house.

My mother's sister, Aunt Claire, and her husband would drop by a couple of times a week. My grandmother was there frequently, and my father's sisters also lived near us. We grew up playing with our cousins and the kids on the block.

Throughout those years, I went my own way. I knew what I wanted—to be independent, successful, well-off, and living a full life—and I set out to get it. I was fortunate to attend the renowned Weequahic High School in Newark, where a lot of kids like me were bent on getting a good education so they could get ahead. But after my sophomore year, my parents bought a house in Union Township, a suburb of New York City. I was not happy.

In Newark, I'd walked everywhere I wanted to go. In Union, I was stranded without a car. Things improved when I got a vehicle in my senior year, but I still missed the city.

Through it all, I learned that I could navigate pretty much anything life threw at me, and that if I did it with confidence, I could usually be successful.

Life Lesson (LL): If you are confident, life is good. Confidence comes from a desire to be the best, and from the innocence of not realizing life's perils. So, go get 'em, and don't think about it.

CHAPTER 2

Rutgers and the Catskills

By the time I got to Rutgers University, where I majored in economics, I was pretty sure I wanted to be an entrepreneur. It was the path of independence I was striving for. I wasn't just a straight-A student; I was also developing business concepts. They never got off the ground, but they were great practice.

One of my ideas was a restaurant called *The Apple Barrel,* with apple-themed dishes like apple pie, apple dumplings, apple fritters, and cinnamon, raisin, and walnut baked apples with cream, along with a full menu of other "comfort food" dishes, but with apples as the star menu attraction. I drew up the plans, designed the restaurant, and went into quite a bit of detail on every aspect of the business. The creativity of the project sparked me.

I also developed an idea for a big balloon with a monster head at each end, which I called Twonster, the two-headed monster.

I believe I was attracted to the life of an entrepreneur, not just because I wanted to be autonomous, but also because I'd been influenced by working with my father. I used to help him load and unload the truck, delivering cases of thirty dozen eggs weighing about forty or forty-five pounds. I saw the customers, what they did, and how they treated my father, who was also a handball champion. He may have been difficult and oppressive at home, but he was well-liked in the community, where he was a local hero.

I thoroughly enjoyed the feeling of community. Clearly, doing this kind of business was different from focusing on making money and moving paper around in some high-rise in the city; this was about people, handshakes, and growing something that mattered. However, at that time in the 1960s, I was also enamored with the idea of being a big shot in a corporate environment. Corporations were just coming into their own in a gilded age of growth and prosperity.

I was on a track to do well at school. I was a Henry Rutgers Scholar, I had my friends, I had my part-time work, and I was moving forward on that particular track. It didn't occur to me to veer off it. Instead, I was determined to do well with what was right in front of me.

I learned almost as much during the summers as I did during school semesters, but the lessons were different. For four summers, I worked as a waiter at large resorts in the Catskill Mountains. That was where I studied the rules and learned how to make them work for me to increase my efficiency.

One waiter could serve forty people a multi-course dinner. The first course was usually a sliced melon, already on the table. The second course was an appetizer, then soup, then the main course, and finally, dessert. In order to serve that many people, you had to be on your toes. I was, and I had a busboy who cleaned up after me.

It was essential to get the courses out efficiently because everyone was looking at other tables to see how fast they were getting their food. The kiss of death occurred when one table would order a plate of sliced tomatoes. Then your table would order the same thing, but we had a rotation, a system. If my table ordered a plate of tomatoes, it would throw me off my system because I'd have to go to another pick-up station.

My way around that? As soon as I noticed another table getting tomatoes, I would order the tomatoes the next time I walked into the kitchen, because I fully expected my people to order them. So, I had them ready.

I was one step ahead and could avoid standing in line at the salad section to get my tomatoes. If I did have to get into line for an extra dish, I was in danger of losing my place in line for the soup or the entrée.

Some people would take a lot of time making an entrée choice. The first courses were pretty easy; they just came along, but there were perhaps eight choices for the main course. People who browsed carefully through the selection had no idea about my rotation and that I was trying to avoid waiting in line with twelve or thirteen waiters in front of me. The first waiter in line would be getting his second table done before my first table was getting served.

How to solve that problem? The skill was in getting someone to make a choice quickly, so I learned to circumvent the issue of too many options by saying, "The roast beef is on special tonight. Would you like that?"

A large part of my job as a waiter was all about planning, and as each summer came around, I internalized the power of planning well.

Breakfast was different. People would simply drift into the dining room, which was fine, but if people came in small groups, you knew by the time 9:30 rolled around, you were going to be hit by a deluge. With the kitchen closing at 10, that was the busy time.

How do you deal with that? The solution was to make sure all the earlier people were done and had left the dining room. At 9:30, you were starting with a clean slate. Then, the idea was to get the order in fast. One way was to say, "The kitchen will close soon..." I learned quickly how to create an efficient system that avoided logjams and roadblocks.

Waiting wasn't an intellectual job, but it had terrific value. I believe the experience taught me a lot about being on time and finding an optimal way to get things done.

LL: Planning and organization are key attributes to business success. How many people do you know who have great skills, but are a mess because they never plan appropriately?

One day, in the summer of 1963, the resort was packed. It was a particularly hot summer, and people in the city were boiling. Some had air conditioning in one room of their house or apartment, but many had none at all. It was cooler in the Catskill Mountains, and we became an attractive option. Record numbers of people arrived, and we escalated from serving thirty plus people per waiter to forty-five or even fifty. We handled it well except for one problem: not enough soup cups.

One of the owners of the resort, who was in charge of the kitchen, created a new rule: bring back the dirty soup cups right away, bypass the washing station, and the kitchen would fill those cups for the next round of people. If the guests didn't get the first round of soup cups, they were getting a dirty one, and that meant we were serving our customers from used cups, which I thought was unhealthy and disgusting.

So, not only did you want your table to order early, you also wanted them to get their soup cups as soon as possible. My busboy and I figured out our own little ruse. We ordered extra soup on the first round, filled the soup cups we had secretly stored, and then poured a little bit of soup into each extra cup—just enough that a quick glance from the cook or the owner would tell them, "Yup—that's a soup cup someone used. They just didn't finish the last little bit." Our "trick" meant we didn't have to wait for our first table to finish.

When I got to the soup station for my second round, the owner just looked at me. "How did you get back here so fast?"

"Well," I said. "The people ate fast. The crowds are really big, so I'm just grabbing the cups before they even finish."

The owner looked at me and raised his eyebrows.

I looked back, my eyes full of unjustified innocence.

I'm sure he didn't believe me for one minute.

I didn't care. It worked. I had a problem, and I'd solved it by thinking outside the proverbial box. I've found in my life that when I'm pushed to be creative, I often do my best.

LL: I think that if you open your horizons and look at unconventional ideas, you'll amaze yourself with what you can create.

The beginning of the annual season at the resort was usually pretty slow. In June, you might have only 20 or 25 people to look after. Of course, that meant fewer tips. But Barry, one of the waiters, was getting 38 people the first week and 38 again the second week. I asked Barry what was going on. He told me truthfully that he was giving the hostess, the sister of the owner, a kickback.

She was tired, hated the job, but needed the money. It still wasn't right, so I approached her and said, "What you're doing isn't right."

She fired me.

But I didn't stay fired. We had a group of three tables belonging to perhaps fifteen couples who rented cabins for the whole season every year. They were wealthy and consequently, influential. Their waiter, Max, probably spilled the beans to them that I'd been fired and why. They immediately told the woman who'd fired me that what she'd done was wrong, and I was instantly rehired.

On August 5 that year, Max had to go home suddenly, and I took over waiting on his three tables of super-tippers, who also happened to be really nice.

LL: Telling my truth and confronting an unjust issue paid off. I never forgot that. It's not enough to just have strong values; you also have to act on them. You have to stand up for what you believe.

Along with being both a Henry Rutgers Scholar and a Woodrow Wilson Scholar at Rutgers, I was also a Phi Beta Gamma, and prided myself on my honesty and integrity. Because Rutgers was a liberal arts college, I also took a class in art history. One day, we had a surprise test. When the instructor announced it, I had a moment of panic and flipped the book open to the section we were being tested on.

The instructor spotted me. I closed the book and took the test. "See me after," he said. When I approached him as the other students filed out of the room, he said, "You cheated. I'm not going to prosecute you for this. I will leave your mark blank."

I felt my heart sink. I was shocked. I thought of myself as an honorable student, but when I'd been ambushed with a surprise test I hadn't prepared for, I'd lost my values.

I was used to other people looking at my papers surreptitiously and cheating by copying my answers, but I'd never thought of doing that myself. I was the best student in statistics, simply because I grasped the subject, and people knew that. Years later, I met a lawyer who had been a fellow student. One of the first things he said to me was, "Hey! Thanks so much for getting me through statistics!"

LL: But that day of the pop quiz, I was mortified. I had violated an image I had of myself, and learned an important lesson about how easily your values can falter if you don't guard them and hold yourself up to the standard you've set.

I was a confident, assertive person, but I had one Achilles heel. When I joined a fraternity, Sigma Alpha Mu (Sammy), I felt unexpectedly unsettled. I was unsure about getting in, and when I was accepted, I continued to doubt myself. Did I belong here? After graduating, members of the fraternity went on to fill prestigious roles in society. Could I measure up to that?

But some people in the fraternity weren't totally honest. One cheated often and was even proud of it. He paid for it later when he became a lawyer, gambled too much and not with his own money, and was disbarred.

The group I socialized with was a bit quieter, although we also had our share of "wise guys." I made friends there, but I still felt self-conscious and perhaps out of my depth. I was used to feeling confident in any situation. Now, suddenly, I felt vulnerable, and it wasn't a comfortable feeling.

Perhaps my bravado had been a cover for this newfound vulnerability. I felt it before I was chosen for the fraternity, hoping I would be selected, but not knowing for sure. I felt it again during the pledging period.

There is a part of everyone that is vulnerable, and now I was discovering that part in myself. I suspect I only got in marginally because one fraternity brother strongly advocated for me. And so, I was being judged, and I didn't like it. What if I were rejected?

I like to think of myself as being perfect. I probably felt that way, too, back in college. Of course, perfection is unattainable, but I strove for it regardless. If I wanted something badly enough, I knew I could do it. But here I was, wanting something—to be accepted into a fraternity—and I had no control over the outcome. I had to depend on the decisions of others, and that made me far too vulnerable.

LL: To the casual observer, we can look perfectly put together and in charge, but do we really know what is going on inside the hearts and minds of the people who look like they have the answer to everything?

I lived off-campus for a couple of years. My two roommates and I lived in the bottom half of a duplex, and we learned to play bridge. The people upstairs also played, so we'd go upstairs starting at about 11 p.m., playing for a penny a point.

In time, we were down about $130, and I was determined to wipe that out. On the last day before graduation, as we were leaving the apartment, my future wife, Marion, was waiting for me, but I was still playing bridge with these guys, trying to lower the amount we owed them. Of course, I ended up paying.

LL: Clearly, I had not yet learned about knowing when to give up.

I met Marion on the beach in August 1964. We got engaged in May 1965 in my senior year, and we were married that September.

My mother was not impressed. My wife's father was also in the egg business, but he had started as a farmer, and in my mother's opinion, was not of the same "station" as our family. She'd had much higher hopes for her "Prince Charming," who was about to enter graduate school. In her opinion, my wife was just an "ordinary girl."

I didn't bat an eye. I was in love and, of course, I knew better than my parents.

My ordinary girl became a teacher, was an adjunct professor at Rutgers, and came into business as my partner, where she was integral to our success. We had a wonderful marriage. She was an exceptionally poised and beautiful woman, even into her eighties.

LL: Judging others without basis can be harmful, as my wife always remembered my mother's view of her during our engagement.

CHAPTER 3

Graduate School

Marion and I got married twice. Why? Well, it was 1965, and "living together" was generally frowned upon, certainly by Marion's mother, who rented two apartments for us in Pittsburgh, where I was about to enroll in the University of Pittsburgh Katz Graduate School of Business. I'd also considered Columbia, but Pittsburgh offered a full scholarship for the one-year program, and that sealed my choice.

Marion and I settled down together in only one of the two apartments. With the fall semester beginning at the end of August, we rented a U-Haul trailer to take our possessions from New York to Pittsburgh, but the hitch or the connection was faulty, and the trailer decoupled so often that a four-hour drive took twelve exhausting hours.

The apartment was tiny: a kitchen and a common area with a Murphy bed, but it suited us just fine. Our first wedding day was September 11, 1965, at City Hall. To celebrate, we rode the tram to Lamont, a restaurant on top of a hill. We had no money, but we scraped together enough to toast the occasion and our happiness with a drink.

On October 31, we got married again, this time in a religious Jewish ceremony and with the blessings of Marion's parents. Shortly before the ceremony, we had a fight—not a lover's spat—but a fight so big it felt like the official wedding was not going to happen. It did. As of the day of writing this, we've been married for almost sixty years, and I have no idea what we fought about.

I worked part-time as a shoe salesman, making about $25 a week, augmenting Marion's salary of $4,800 per year, which was our main source of income. We had to be careful with our money if we didn't want to go into debt, but my shoe salesman's earnings was our fun money, the best money of the week.

We would treat ourselves to a dinner out, or a special luxury food at the grocery store, or a new shirt or sweater. We had so much fun spending that money. It made us happy, and every week we anticipated our little treat. The rest of the week, we got by just watching our expenses carefully. Unexpected bills weren't a part of our tight budget. One day, Marion contracted a virus and had to visit the doctor. We counted our money carefully to cover it.

At the supermarket, we added up our purchases as we put them in the cart. One night a week, we ate hot dogs, one night it was chicken livers, and another it was chuck steak, the cheapest cut we could find.

But one night a week, we'd go out with Joe Betty, one of the most special people I've ever known. I met Joe in one of my classes, and we simply hit it off. He was a staunch Catholic with a deep, unshakeable faith. He had just left the Peace Corps and lived in a small, plain bachelor apartment, a large cross hanging over his bed. It wasn't his belief in God that struck me, but his faith in humanity. I was so much more practical and business-oriented than he was. In fact, I even wondered why he was studying for his MBA.

Joe embodied the meaning of authentic. He was altruistic, kind, and utterly genuine. Our relationship was special, and I believe that even then, I knew how rare it was to meet a dedicated believer. Once a week, he and Marion, and I would go to a restaurant that served a chicken dinner for sixty cents and a beer for twenty-five cents.

Joe was one of a number of exceptional people I met. I believe most teachers are special, vastly underrated by our society. My wife introduced me to her friends and continued to do so over the years. All that time, I have truly enjoyed their company. They tended to be as interested in my businesses and enterprises as I was in their professions. Partly through them, I learned to appreciate people whose backgrounds were not the same as mine, and to cultivate their friendships.

We had five or six Iranians in our class who knew each other and generally kept to themselves, but were happy to socialize with the rest of us. They were lovely people with a great sense of humor. I appreciated knowing them, and that they were here in the United States to further their education.

LL: I think we are sometimes unfair to our foreign students and foreigners in general. They come from different cultures. Knowing and accepting them can broaden our own outlook on the world and open our minds to new ideas.

I believe I graduated first in my class, and it wasn't necessarily an easy ride. I had one instructor teaching advanced math who gave us a test one day on everything we didn't know and hadn't studied. We could not have prepared for it, and it was far beyond our skill set. While we were bent over our papers, sweating in fear and confusion, the instructor walked up and down the aisles, snapping pencils with his hands.

I was a good student—an excellent student even—but the questions I was being asked might as well have been written in Greek.

"Are you guys having a hard time?" the instructor goaded.

Another pencil snapped.

I was not thrilled with the results of my test: 43%, but the instructor gave me a B-plus. I believe that was the highest mark in the class. The test may have seemed bizarre, but he was teaching us a lesson.

LL: Sometimes adverse conditions come at you unexpectedly, and you just have to deal with them.

The highlight, or possibly lowlight, of my year at the Pittsburgh Katz Graduate School of Business was a market research course taught by a visiting professor from Stanford. I found his hypotheses weird, including his comparison of market research to AC/DC currents. Up to that point, I'd been getting straight As. This last course was the one from hell. To graduate, we had to write a major thesis. I stalled, preferring to while away my time that hot summer in the university's pool rather than hunched down over my books.

The proposition I finally settled on was that blue-collar families tended to be more brand loyal than white collar families. Marion was off work for the summer and offered to help. We went out to shopping centers to talk to consumers. My results were coming in with no definitive conclusions. However, Marion's results completely bore out my hypothesis.

"Wow!" I said. "You had the right set of people. What happened? We're at the same shopping center!"

She smiled and said, "Well, I'm a good interviewer."

And the light bulb went on in my head. She was skewing the results with the questions she was asking.

LL: I never forgot that lesson. Now, whenever I read market research polls, or interviews and comments, I carefully peruse the details and statistical analyses, and look at the questions and all their nuances. They can seriously skew the results.

The professor gave me a B, saying, "Okay. I don't really believe this, but..."

I just said, "Thank you."

My work was done, and I was happy to move on to my next step: getting a job.

CHAPTER 4

A Corporate Job and the National Guard

E ven though I had an entrepreneurial soul, I was intent on getting a job in the corporate world. Back then, it was highly desirable because everyone wanted a good position working for a major corporation, and I was driven to do well in that arena.

I'd already had several interviews and had a job offer at the University of California as an economics instructor. I gave it serious thought. A college in Pennsylvania also offered me a teaching position, which I also considered. But then I had an interview with Lever Brothers in New York, one of the highest-ranked, prestigious marketing companies in America. That was the job I coveted.

They flew me to New York, where I interviewed with a number of managers. I completed some tests and then went to lunch at a fine French restaurant with the manager who had the authority to hire me.

I ordered a Crenshaw melon to start, served on a coupe of ice. I purposefully dug my spoon into the melon, which levitated alarmingly and flew across the table, landing on my potential boss' tie with a quiet splat.

I did not get the job.

I did get the next job I interviewed for with S&H Green Stamps as an acquisitions and corporate development specialist. I was the junior of two acquisitions analysts, working for a manager. Above him was the vice president of the department. The latter liked me a lot, while the former was focused more on company politics than getting results.

Located on Madison Avenue in New York City, S&H was a marketing promotions company that sold stamps to supermarkets and other major retailers who gave them to their customers when they checked out. The customers pasted the stamps into books, which they redeemed for prizes like toasters, vacuum cleaners, or televisions, depending on the number of books they turned in.

For years, the stamps had been immensely popular, but were beginning to die out when I joined the company. S&H had a redemption rate of about 85%, but kept a liability of 100% on its balance sheet. As a result, they had about $350 million cash in unredeemed stamp liability. They were also generating about $30 million a year in cash. In today's world, this represents several billion dollars in funds with bank financing.

I started my job at the end of August, right after graduating. I had enough money to buy one blue pin-striped suit from Brooks Brothers for $65. Then, after putting down a deposit on an apartment in New Jersey, Marion and I were out of money. To give us a small cushion while we waited for our first paychecks, I got a Labour Day weekend job as a waiter at a New Jersey resort. Between salary and tips, I knew we'd be okay.

On my way to my first shift at the resort on Friday night, I dropped my suit off at the dry cleaners and picked it up again before my shift on Saturday. I made several hundred dollars that weekend and put on my suit on Tuesday morning to go to work. But when I opened the dry cleaner's bag, I saw the jacket, but no pants.

Somewhere between home and the dry cleaner, they'd slipped off the hanger, and they were gone. I had an interview that morning with the large consulting firm, Booz Allen, to discuss some acquisition prospects. I did the best I could, putting on a pair of grey wool herringbone pants and my pinstriped blue jacket and tie.

I went to the interview, where I determined that the representative for Booz Allen didn't have a lot to offer, and went back to the office. After work, I bought another suit.

A few days later, the vice president summoned me into his office. "I need to talk to you about how to dress," he said.

LL: I said nothing. I instinctively knew that if you tell a long story, it doesn't help you; it only makes it worse. I took my lumps.

A key function of my job was doing analyses of companies and industries, conducting either personal interviews or relying on market research. I made use of services that assembled data to use in my evaluations, and became a good researcher, gaining tremendous experience in organizing the data. That, combined with what I had learned in school and at my job in the Catskills, stood me in good stead. I studied many different companies and industries, and even though I was a junior, I was sent out to interview a number of potential acquisitions.

I was a year and a half into the job, and nothing was happening; no acquisitions and none before that when my department was first created. The division wasn't doing what it was supposed to. Then we began studying a company in Chicago that produced shows or presentations for corporations. One of their clients was the Ford Motor Company. When they introduced a new car, the company would put on a glittering production. Our analysis was positive. It was public and profitable.

We flew out to Chicago and worked on the proposal. We had no doubt this was a good one. We created a presentation, preparing to show it to the board. A few days later, we were standing outside the boardroom, waiting for the results of the presentation and the board's approval.

At the last possible minute, one person on the board said no.

And that was it. No acquisition. More than anything else, it was embarrassing for our department and for the company. This should have been easy. A simple rubber stamp of the proposal. Our department still showed no deals.

Three months later, one of the bankers on the board brought us Bigelow Carpets as an acquisition. The deal was completed in three days. I suspect it went through quickly because of our previous embarrassment, and also because we had someone championing the deal.

LL: On acquisitions, mergers, or new ventures and ideas, you need a significant supporter.

After that, we bought an office furniture company, and another home and office furnishings company.

I worked at S&H for two and a half years. They treated me well and gave me very acceptable raises. I started at $12,000, and by the time I left, I was making $20,000 per year; an excellent salary at that time.

Every morning, I would take the 7:50 train into the city with three other regulars, and while we chugged along, we would play bridge. The winning team at the end of the ride got two dollars. But the trick was, we didn't shuffle the cards. After a hand was played, we'd just put the cards back together and deal them out again. It made for some interesting lopsided hands, and even more interesting playing of the hands. I loved it. If I could make the 5:30 train home, we'd play again.

LL: I have no idea if I learned anything from that experience, other than if something brings you joy, go for it! Try it!

Another significant event occurred during those years at S&H. When I left graduate school, the army was calling people up for the Vietnam War. However, if you volunteered for the National Guard, you did your duty, but the odds were excellent that you would not be shipped overseas. If you didn't want to fight in the war, the National Guard was a good alternative.

I wound up in a National Guard tank unit. Six months after starting my job at S&H, I was called up to basic training at Fort Knox. My big issue was that my glasses had broken and I was struggling to see, and that worried me. The rumor was that if you didn't pass basic training, you would be shipped to Vietnam, and I had to pass the rifle shooting test. When the day came, I was close to panicking, especially because I had done poorly in the practice rounds. To my relief, I passed as a middle-level shooter. I have no idea how, but I did.

LL: There is a god. But, in fact, I was well trained, and the training paid off.

After eight weeks at basic, I spent another eight weeks at Fort Dix in New Jersey at tank school. One recruit there was a bit of a nerd—heavy set, glasses, not very strong—an easily forgettable guy. But he started a company that routed faxes anywhere they needed to go. His concept was ingenious and successful.

LL: It's a tired old cliché to say, "Never judge a book by its cover," but old as it is, it's also usually true.

With training complete, I put in one weekend a month for additional training. I was designated a medic, even though I had trained as a tank driver. However, I did take courses every time I went for training. I believe I was the only one without some kind of medical background. But when we were given a proficiency test, I was the only one who passed. It was simple, really: in the multiple-choice test, I came up with the right answers by a straightforward process of deduction.

In July 1967, 158 riots erupted in urban communities across America, including in Newark, sparked by a dispute between Black citizens and white police officers that escalated to violence. They resulted in 83 deaths and 17,000 arrests. Property damage in Newark was estimated at $115 million.

My unit was called up. We were in Newark at a waiting station and not deployed, but we were ready to move in. Other units went, some with live ammunition, and one guardsman fired at a resident for no reason. We were not properly trained to handle the situation.

LL: You may be thrust into strange and even frightening events that you have no control over. Be aware of them and deal with them.

Every summer, often in May, our unit was sent to camp for active training in upstate New York for two weeks. We'd drive up for six or eight hours and pitch pup tents for sleeping and larger tents for cooking and dining.

I hated being there and did my best to figure out a way to beat the system. I would volunteer for the easy duties and get in the back of the line for anything that resembled hard work. Sometimes I'd just disappear. I became a master at beating the system.

In the fifth year of camp, we stayed in barracks for the last four days. One day, we were hanging around, and one of the guys said to me, "Wolf, we have your number. You shirk everything."

What was he saying?

I turned to our platoon leader, who I knew was a good and fair person. "Is that true?"

"It is."

I was shocked, not that I was shirking, but that I'd been caught at my game. I went home and thought about it. The next summer, my sixth, I went back to camp, but this time I was determined to be present, to volunteer, and not try to "get away" with anything. I was going to fully participate.

Surprise! I had a great time.

LL: I learned a valuable lesson that year. Handle what's in front of you, and whatever the situation is, participate. Be there. It works better to make the best of what you've got.

At the end of my stint with S&H Green Stamps, I was ready for my first entrepreneurial experience. I especially remember my vice president, Mr. Mills, with great fondness. The company had given me great training to prepare me for my next step.

CHAPTER 5

Scientific Restaurant Management Corporation

I n 1968, the stock market was doing well, so I saw an opportunity to do a roll-up, a process used by investors where multiple small companies are acquired and merged. On my own time, I started looking at restaurants for sale, and found The Jolly Troll, a low-priced smorgasbord restaurant, based in Minneapolis. Swedish-oriented, it was definitely a smorgasbord, and not a buffet.

My wife's uncle, Jerry, an accountant with Arthur Anderson, one of the top accounting firms in the country at the time, partnered with me. He was a terrific guy, nine years my senior, and excited about going into business. I was also excited, but I was only twenty-six (a young Turk as they called those eager for change in those days) and not with as much experience as Jerry.

We named our company Scientific Restaurant Management Corporation, and found a small investment banker to raise the capital we needed: $600,000 in equity. But as the deal was ready to close, the banker offered us only $450,000, of which $300,000 was subordinated debt, and $150,000 was equity. Obviously, the deal was no longer as attractive, but we were standing at the finish line, so The Jolly Troll became our first acquisition.

I was less concerned about the quality of the restaurant acquisitions and more focused on finding deals quickly and putting them together. The Jolly Troll had seven company-owned restaurants. Our idea was to franchise it. We also wanted to issue stock and take the company public as quickly as possible. That would raise more capital, but I had also learned in my stint with S&H that a good many people like being part of a public company. They feel they have ownership in it, and more than that, it makes them feel important.

I also discovered that being an entrepreneur can be lonely. While you are the boss, no one really gives you recognition, or if they do, it's all from the bottom up, and then it's easy to brush those compliments off as toadying. If you are associated with a bigger group, you can feel valuable and valued.

This is why people gravitate to groups. Today's clearest example is the internet, where you can find people with unusual or radical views, seeking out and joining groups who think the way they do. Not only are their views validated, but they also get that feeling of importance.

The Jolly Troll restaurants offered low-priced meals: $1.79 for dinner and $1.29 for lunch. All you can eat. The spaces were decorated with happy trolls working in the kitchen or at different stations in the restaurant. Children loved it.

But there was a problem. The concept only worked in large communities, and most particularly, in areas with a sizeable Swedish population. Swedish people tended to like buffet dining. Others did too, but not sustainably. For them, it was a novelty.

This meant there was no growth potential, and gradually, business decreased. In time, we closed a number of the restaurants. We opened two more Jolly Trolls in New Jersey, but we faced the same issues there: large sales initially, followed by a decline. Another problem: it took an extraordinary manager to handle quality control. Bottom line: it was not a good concept in terms of management or marketing.

However, we had two profitable restaurants in Seattle and Minneapolis, both with a large Swedish population. The rest, although not losing great swaths of money, were still losing. Regardless, I wanted to keep moving on, making more acquisitions. We bought a seafood restaurant in New Jersey where the owner was leaving and the chef was stepping up to become the new manager. Then we also opened a steakhouse in New Jersey. That gave us four restaurants within the first two years of our partnership.

Obviously, money was tight, and it cost a fair bit to open and run the restaurants. So, we had a few bucks in the bank and a $300,000 loan.

I quickly learned that going into partnership with someone whose philosophy is different from your own can be fraught. My partner, Jerry, with his accounting background and a substantial house on the line, was concerned about the loan he had personally guaranteed and about the money we were losing. On top of that were the daily expenditures in upkeep and the aggravation of staffing and hiring. This became particularly apparent with our star chef/manager, who was married, had just had a baby, and ran off with the hostess, never to be seen again.

He was gone, and he was our cornerstone for that restaurant. We never did replace him satisfactorily.

In 1971, Jerry insisted on bankrupting the company. We did. Then we paid the loan back to the bank in full, and paid off all our vendors in full. Technically, it was a bankruptcy, but in reality, we simply shut it down. No one suffered, except perhaps me, just a bit. I was never able to fully implement my strategy. On the other hand, Jerry was never able to have a conservatively financed business that was consistently making money.

LL: My advice? Don't go into business with a relative if you are not in control, and especially, don't go into business with someone who has a different philosophy from yours.

There were other lessons for me in this enterprise. We sold a lot of chicken in our buffets. In New Jersey, the price for the chicken was cheap, but what we didn't realize was that the vendor was packing the chicken in ice and underweighting it. One day, we pulled the chicken out of the ice and weighed it.

Oh!

LL: Another lesson learned: if you want to do well in business, you have to pay attention, and when things appear to be too good to be true, they are.

And another lesson: the price for dinner in our restaurant on the Jersey Shore was $1.99. Five percent tax brought it to $2.09, but Jerry thought that rather than giving people a penny in change, we'd round it up to $2.10. What's a penny, right?

It turned out a penny was a lot. Two weeks after "rounding things up," customers noticed and began to complain. "What's going on here? It's supposed to be $2.09!"

We had no leg to stand on and started charging the proper percentage: $2.09.

LL: Honestly? If you're going to cheat, make sure you don't get caught— and you will get caught. Even better? Don't cheat. Not even by a penny.

Maybe letting go of the business wasn't such a bad thing. I was exhausted. I'd find myself cooking, running around, working late hours, and rushing to do anything that needed doing. But my concept had been destroyed. How might it all have been different if we had dug in and stuck with the original idea?

In the end, I conceded. I wasn't in a position to go it alone. From Jerry's point of view, it was too risky, and I could understand that. He had put his house on the line when he signed for the loan.

And me? I'd gained valuable experience, and I was ready to move on.

CHAPTER 6

Cheesy Business

I was a driven guy and quickly found a job as manager of acquisitions and mergers with Brooke Bond Foods Inc. in Lake Success near Queens, New York. I followed the procedures I knew well by now, looking at businesses and assessing whether we wanted to buy them.

I started making acquisitions in the cheese industry. Brooke Bond Foods' parent company, Brooke Bond Liebig, based in London, England, and a subsidiary in Canada that had a cheese business (Black Diamond), had a fair bit of interest in cheese. I looked at a lot of industries, visiting fifty or sixty food businesses before settling on a company in Philadelphia that my boss, who was far too cost-conscious, considered affordable. It was doing about $20 million in sales, and we bought it for about $2 million. Shortly after that, we bought a cheese company in Wisconsin doing about $5 million in sales for about $500,000.

We also started importing about $1 million worth of cheese from Canada, as well as other specialty cheeses from Denmark. Our three specialty cheese divisions consisted of Denmark, Canada, and a business we developed that consisted of cheese scraps mixed with grain that we sold to dog food manufacturers. They were all nicely profitable.

The business in Philadelphia was doing well, but the owner we bought it from retired, and that's when the problems began. The new management was a small disaster. Cheese is a low-margin business, but in any business, you have to watch for "leakage"—any place you lose margin—and management in Philadelphia wasn't doing that.

Meanwhile, the company in Wisconsin was losing money, but our boss wanted higher sales. We could say we were doing $25 million in sales, while Brooke Bond Foods itself was only doing $25 million, mainly in the coffee and spice business. In other words, with Wisconsin on board, we were doubling the size of our company, but the margins were not working, becoming significantly negative.

With the acquisitions completed, the Brooke Bond Foods CEO approached me with, "I want you to be my eyes and ears. Go down to Philadelphia and Wisconsin and tell us what's going on."

When I came back, I told him, "This place is a disaster. People are not doing their jobs. They're not following through. The margins are bad, and there's a lot of politics."

"Okay," he said. "You run it."

At age thirty, I took over the business and moved it from $25 million in sales to about $55 million in two plus years, employing a lot of my own ideas.

When I arrived, I could best describe the Wisconsin management as haphazard, making a lot of cheese that was substandard. That meant they had about $500,000 in cheese that didn't make the grade. That was called "rework." Most of the cheese we sold was American in five-pound loaves that were then sliced at the deli counter. Our major market was Philadelphia, which used white American cheese. In New York, we sold the same cheese, but it was colored yellow. Boston was white, Chicago was yellow, and Maryland was white. Why? Who knows? That was just the way it was. Our stock of rework was yellow.

We could add about 5 percent rework to our blend, cook it, and come out with white American cheese. We had a lot of rework, so my boss said, "Why don't we move the rework from 5 percent to 6 percent?"

I said, "I don't know."

He said, "Trust me, I did this in the coffee business."

It worked.

Then he suggested 7 percent rework, and then 8 percent.

We had a huge order at that time for Acme Supermarkets for 1.5 million pounds of white American cheese. We added 250,000 pounds of rework to the order. The cheese came out striated, white with yellow streaks. We had to reject all of it and turn it back into rework. It took more than a year to use it all up.

We should never have let a boss who didn't know about the cheese business talk us into his greedy idea. It backfired big time.

LL: If you believe in something, stick with it.

We had other problems in Philadelphia and Wisconsin involving management. I learned pretty quickly that when you see a lot of closed-door meetings, it's a very bad sign. I'm a strong believer in open-door meetings.

LL: Closed doors only lead to trouble, especially when those meetings happen all day long.

We did good business in Philadelphia, selling American cheese to supermarkets like Acme and Wawa Food Stores. We also sold them ten-pound loaves of provolone, Munster, cheddar, and Swiss cheese to use in their deli. Medium-sized distributors would come to our plant to pick up product, or we would deliver locally to the distributors.

So, I had an idea. I opened a warehouse in a cost-effective Quonset hut we rented in Brooklyn. I staffed it with a manager and stocked it with a variety of cheeses. We were located next to Boar's Head Provisions, whose independent truck distributors would come over regularly to buy our cheeses, which we called New Yorker Cheese. We quickly built up a $15-$20 million business there over two years.

Main Street Cheese was our competitor, and he let us do it without a fight. I couldn't help wondering, "Why didn't they open a distribution center in Philadelphia?" By having a physical distribution center, we proved we were in business. Sure, we could say we had products and we'd deliver them, but we were right there.

Look at Amazon today. Part of their success is based on, "You want it? You got it!"

LL: What I understood was that if you want to be in business, you have to show yourself. It didn't cost a lot to set up that Quonset hut, and it paid off.

I learned business-to-business (BtoB) marketing, not only the mechanics of it, but also its importance. A lot of today's millionaires, who are not in the tech sector, are doing BtoB. They're selling widgets, light bulbs, parts, and pieces; a million different things that other businesses and manufacturers need. And in fact, some of the most highly valued tech companies make the components, not the end product.

To sell our products, I concentrated on sales literature and brochures that we delivered to retailers, restaurants, or schools. I'm pretty sure I was one of the early adopters to recognize and understand that market. The philosophy is simple: a lot of these people want to feel important, recognized, and seen.

LL: To be successful in BtoB marketing, you have to build personal relationships and make your customers feel important.

Our plant in Wisconsin was making chunks of cheese for supermarkets and doing a modest amount of business. So, I put together a marketing campaign that said, "We put your good name on our good name."

We sent our supermarket buyers personalized gifts like coffee mugs with their individual names on them, letter openers, paper holders, and several others. Each gift was personalized with the buyer's name and came with sales literature. That campaign brought us a number of large customers.

We also had a close relationship with a sales agency in New York who was our broker, and we wanted to make the sales agents work harder for us. My wife and I lived on Long Island now, and we invited the agents to our house for a grand dinner.

LL: Business relationships that involve making your customer, client, or organization's employees feel wanted, respected, and important are a strong key to success.

Not all my efforts were a home run. One time, I had a meeting with a management consultant who was going to have a look at our business in Philadelphia. We set up a meeting at a restaurant in New York City. We settled on one, and then mentioned another one instead. I went to the second one we'd talked about. He went to the first one. After waiting forty-five minutes, the light dawned.

Uh oh.

I tore over to the other restaurant, and he was furious. Nothing I could say or do could mend that particular fence. He never spoke to me again. Mistakes happen, and sometimes you can do nothing about them to make them right.

LL: Sometimes, you just have to let it go.

In the middle of all this "cheesy business," I put together a theory that the fifties were the era of marketing; the sixties were all about finance and organizing; and the seventies were an era of scarcer resources, and the food companies that knew how to use those resources would do well.

At that time, I had a job interview with Morgan Stanley as their food analyst, which would certainly prove my theory. The analyst's job was to present his findings to mutual funds. At that time, the mutual funds traded through the brokerage houses, which made a commission. The analysts were important to the success of the brokerage houses. I was absolutely up for doing the job. I had my hair razor cut, put on my best suit, polished my shoes, and even did my research by going to the library to prepare for the psychological test I had to take.

I looked over some old tests, and it turned out that the one I was given was the same as that from the late 1950s that I had studied in detail. Wow! I was all set to get a perfect score.

When I finished and handed in my paper, the psychologist said, "You rigged the test. Your score was perfect. Each characteristic was 100 or 0 percent."

I said, "Well, I did, in a way."

More tests followed, including a lie detector test. Why so many tests?

And then they kept saying, "You're going to make so much money. Don't worry about it."

Okay, but why did they feel the need to repeat that so often? Something about this didn't feel right.

I got the job.

Then I entered my boss' office at Brooke Bond Foods to tell him I was quitting.

He asked me to stay, and I did. Why? Yes, I got a raise, but that wasn't the deciding point. I would have made a million dollars a year or more at Morgan Stanley. Why did I make that decision? Instinct?

I once said to my wife, "I wonder what would have happened if I had taken that job?"

"What do you mean? You never would have started Alpine Lace!"

Well then. That's a nice and simple answer.

LL: Go with your instinct.

So, I stayed, and about a year later, I was fired. Two things happened, but both boiled down to one thing: mentor/mentee conflict. First, a stuffy, self-important bigwig flew over from the parent company in England. I flew with him to Wisconsin to visit the plant there, and right after sitting down beside him on the plane, I spotted a friend a few rows back and excused myself, saying I wanted to chat with my buddy. I left him and sat with my friend for almost the entire flight. London Bigwig thought I was unforgivably rude. And yes, I suppose I was.

The second thing involved my boss' son, who worked for me but was doing something out of line. I called him in and suggested I might have to let him go.

Right after that, my boss fired me. Those two incidents were the obvious reasons. What was really at the heart of it was the change in the mentor/mentee relationship. I'd outgrown my mentor, and the friction was becoming obvious.

LL: The relationship between a mentor and mentee can only survive for so long. Inevitably, the mentee will outgrow the role.

It was time for me to break away.

CHAPTER 7

Interlude, Turnaround, and Instincts

S uddenly, I was between jobs, but I started looking and immediately got an offer to run a distribution business in New Jersey. I was slightly uneasy, because rather than working with a brand, I'd be employed by a distribution company. I was also a bit on edge because the owner had recently died, leaving his wife and two children in charge.

The company ran about forty tractor-trailer trucks, delivering bread to about eighty McDonald's locations, and a variety of bread and baked goods to 120 Pathmark stores, a mega-supermarket chain in New Jersey, Pennsylvania, and the New York metropolitan area.

The late owner had had a good friendship with his two principal customers, and his wife was rightly concerned about how his passing would affect the company, which was already losing money.

When I came in, I had a good look at how the business was operating, taking charge with the intention of bringing it out of the red and into the black. First, I looked at efficiencies. If you're in the distribution business, you want to track how long it takes to make a delivery, how much downtime each driver experiences, and how well the routes are working.

One of the first things I discovered was that the trucks going to Pathmark were rarely full, so I negotiated with the company to deliver other items that would fill the trucks, which quickly became more efficient, and I watched our financials creep up into the black zone.

However, I'd been there two months when McDonald's announced it was about to make a change in its operations and would start bringing in bread from its own factories. They gave us three months' notice.

We faced a problem with the impending change. McDonald's paid us within a week, while we paid the bread vendor in three weeks. With McDonald's pulling out, we would lose our cash flow. But we had a number of bread and cake suppliers whose products we sold to Pathmark, so I started slowing down payments to the vendors three months prior to the changeover, moving them back a week. Then we moved them back three weeks. When the supplier complained, we started paying them a day or two sooner. We then paid them on a regular basis, but several weeks later than we had before. As long as we kept paying them, they were happy.

By the time the McDonald's change took effect, we had enough cash flow.

LL: Planning ahead was essential not only to keeping afloat, but also to thriving. And again, the lesson is true that an adverse event can result in a much better outcome.

During those three crucial months, we were also working on getting additional business.

I was certain we were on our way to succeeding, but I was wary of staying in a family-owned and operated business. While they thought I was a hero for making them profitable and seeing them over what could have been a big stumbling block, I was concerned about my future with them.

LL: In the end, family always wins. I had no doubt we would eventually experience friction as they wanted to exert more control. If we didn't agree on a strategy or issue, they would inevitably call the shots.

CHAPTER 8

Standard Brands and Betrayal

S ix months after I started working with the distribution business, I bowed out. But I'd still been looking for a permanent job, and landed one at Standard Brands in New York City, where I immediately found myself in a *Mad Men-style* political corporate environment.

Standard Brands was a publicly-traded company, a conglomerate of various brands including Chase & Sanborn coffee, Planters Peanuts, Fleischmann Yeast, Droste Chocolate, Nips and Baby Ruth Candies, and Royal Puddings. I was hired as manager of new specialty foods, reporting to an extraordinarily political vice president who was also an aggressive ladder-climber. My boss reported to an upper manager I never got along with. He disliked anything and everything I said or suggested. He was older, out of touch with current tastes and marketing, and probably fearful of getting bumped from his job, possibly by my VP. In other words, he was acting out of fear and not strength.

I developed a new herbal tea line called Herbal Tease and a Droste Cocoa that would take advantage of the strong reputation Droste Chocolate from Holland enjoyed. But I realized pretty quickly that the situation, and probably my job, were not going to last. My boss played both sides, keeping me strung along while very likely taking his boss' side against me.

I got fired: the second time in eighteen months, but my depression started before that. Given the stress of the job, it's not surprising. But much more than the rigors of the position, what tipped the scales for me was the fact of being betrayed.

The first time I was fired, I'd grown out of the mentor-mentee relationship, and that was a betrayal of sorts, and now, I'd been double-crossed by an unethical boss. I felt strongly deceived by someone who was supposed to have my back. The truth was, he was a Judas.

The last months on the job, I'd go into work and spend an hour at the breakfast restaurant in the General Motors building across the street. I'd sit there, just building up my psyche to get up, walk back across the street, and face another day at the office. Every day was a struggle.

One day, my sister-in-law happened to enter the restaurant. Oh my God! I did not want to talk to her. I didn't even want her to see me. I was almost shaking with embarrassment.

Medication helped lift me out of the black hole I'd sunk into; that, and time, and the need to find another job.

Only recently, I was listening to a radio program where the owner of a makeup line was being interviewed about a book she had written that chronicled her severe anxiety. She said it was so bad at times, she couldn't function. Her message was that eventually, you just have to plow through it.

LL: You have to plow through it, and you will, even though you don't think you will, you will. You have to go through each day and just get by.

When the signs became clear to me that I was going to be fired, I started looking for another job and interviewed with Gerber Foods in Pennsylvania. Because I was deeply depressed, my voice had fallen, and there was no energy behind my words. The interviewer said many times, "Can you speak louder?"

I did my best, but when I finished the interview, I knew how badly I'd done. "Well," I said to myself. "That was a pretty crappy interview."

And I got the job.

But I didn't take it. I was just starting to feel better and decided to go into business for myself. A year later, Gerber was indicted for adding sugar water to its baby apple juice. I'd like to take credit for being smart enough to avoid the disaster that ensued, but I'll have to chalk it up to luck. Everyone in the company was tarnished with that particular brush.

LL: Sometimes luck really does play a role, or maybe you create your own luck through your instincts.

My decision was to let my entrepreneurial spirit loose.

CHAPTER 9

Entrepreneur, Consultant, Sales Agent, Partner, Trader

I was lucky to have two benefactors when I struck out on my own. One was the Danish cheese company I'd dealt with when I worked with Brooke Bond Foods. They hired me to be their sales agent for the United States. The other, who hired me as a consultant, was the Fmali Herb Company in Santa Cruz, California, with whom I had worked developing an herbal tea brand for Standard Brands.

So, I had an income and two benefactors. I spent a week each month in Santa Cruz with Fmali, helping them run their business. The work allowed me to comfortably set up Market Finders as a sales agent (food broker), mainly in cheese products at the beginning, and Market Cheese Traders, which bought and sold cheese and acted as a sales agent. My wife, Marion, who was an adroit administrator and communicator, also joined me, making it easier for me to focus on being the front man of the operation.

I developed a close relationship with Ben and Louise Zaricor, who owned Fmali. The dominant factor in the business was Ben, a strong, fierce, demanding, and sometimes combative man. Once, we had a shouting match, where my anger flared up so hard, I shoved him, and he shoved me back.

Still, we worked together well enough. I helped him develop his line of herbs, loofahs, and various other products, imported for the most part from China, and that he sold mainly to retailers. He processed the herbs in his plant in Santa Cruz. When I was there several days a month, I initially stayed in the guest house on his property, and then at a local motel on the Pacific Ocean—a beautiful experience. At dawn and dusk, I would look out at the dancing waves, gulls swooping down over the beach, and surfers launching themselves out on their boards. I came to believe that most young people in America in the 1970s spent at least one day of their lives in Santa Cruz, a place to feed the soul.

My work with Fmali was intense. I was involved in all their decision-making and was an integral part of their operations. Fmali created the tea blend for the nine Good Earth restaurants, owned by General Mills. I helped Ben negotiate the rights to the line for retail sales, and a few years later, helped him develop the brand by advertising on local TV stations until Good Earth became a significant brand. Uniquely, Good Earth was regular black tea that needed no sweetening because it contained pungent herbs like cinnamon, orange peel, and cloves.

I also helped Ben hire salespeople and watched Good Earth Tea grow to a $20 million business.

In 1980, we started a partnership that imported Honeyrose herbal cigarettes, made from dried flowers and honey and containing no nicotine. I created a marketing plan that focused heavily on advertising in business trade publications with circulations of 5,000 to 10,000 or more, talking directly to distributors. We hired a professional photographer and produced a glossy, foldout movie-style poster for the magazines, creating an image of success and expertise in our field.

We also hired a public relations agency, which tapped me as the front person to do interviews for all our various markets. Some articles were full or double-page spreads. We were a big hit, garnering millions in publicity value. Newsday on Long Island, however, only did a blurb on us. However, its circulation was about a million, and that small paragraph elicited hundreds of inquiries.

We also hired a husband and wife team who traveled the country in an RV, visiting all the distributors as they went, selling our Honeyrose line to virtually the entire country.

In the end, we had national distribution and received excellent publicity because a number of Hollywood people smoked them, including Jane Fonda. However, we had one major problem. The cigarettes had an absolutely acrid smell, five times as pungent as marijuana. To say the odor was annoying is an understatement. It was even a negative for the smoker.

So, we got the publicity; we got the distribution; and we had a great marketing plan, but the product wasn't great.

LL: My advice? Don't try to sell a product that isn't good. You have to have a good and sustainable product. If you don't, all the advertising in the world is just hype.

While I was doing food brokering with my wife, we went into a joint venture with Ben and Louise, selling their tea to the food services trade, which, in turn, sold it mainly to restaurants. We hired a salesperson, and it worked this way: Good Earth sold us their tea at the wholesale price, and we resold it to the food service trade, developing a $2 million business with a little profit for us. It went well, but it was a lot of work—more than my time was worth—so I gave the business back to them. They never forgave me, because they felt I was giving up our relationship, and as far as they were concerned, I was family. They were deeply hurt.

I think I could have handled it better. I could have paused and perhaps given more thought to my actions and how they might affect them.

LL: Be sensitive to others' thoughts and feelings.

Ben was, as I mentioned earlier, a fierce businessman; so much so that at times I would cringe when I observed his interactions with suppliers, service people, or staff. He could create high tension in a heartbeat. He didn't do it with me, probably because he knew I wouldn't take it, but he was strict and demanding with his salespeople, furious if they didn't achieve or exceed their quotas.

One time, I was helping him negotiate the sale of his business to Celestial Tea. As the front person, I was setting up the deal, but Ben wanted too much and it never went through. Then we hired an investment banker, but Ben wanted an astronomical price for the company, and the banker told him he couldn't get that price. In fact, no one was interested in buying.

However, a few years later, Ben sold Good Earth, including the value of the food services company, to an Indian company at a very substantial price. He never thanked me for the extra value our food service business added to the sale of his company.

LL: Not everyone is like you. They have different values and ways they operate. However, surprise! They may be a success anyway.

Before Ben sold the company, we got the idea to sell Good Earth as a bottled beverage, and hired a consulting firm to develop the recipe as well as a marketing consultant to research manufacturing facilities. I believed the product could do very well because it had enough natural flavor and sweetness that it needed no added sugar. It also contained enough caffeine to give people a boost, and we could add a carbonated version to our product line.

Looking at the possibilities, I told the Zaricors that I believed this new product would be a valuable asset to the company. Corporations like Pepsi-Cola and Coca-Cola were buying up beverage companies, particularly tea companies that had products they could put on their regular distribution routes. To make that happen, we first had to have a co-packer manufacture the product, then put it in retail locations to assess how well it did. I'd always loved this area of the business because it didn't require a lot of marketing expenditures. You just had to put it on the shelf as a virtue product. In other words, people would buy it because they liked the idea of the product. If they took to it, they would buy it again. The product had to taste good and *be* good. In other words, it had to have virtues.

The major cost of getting our bottled teas on store shelves was distribution. If it cost us fifty cents to make and sell, the retail price might be $1.50 – $2, due to the costs of distribution plus retail markup.

LL: The way to make an endeavor like this work is to find a product with virtue, get it into limited distribution, even giving away product, assessing how well it sells, and then making adjustments where needed.

Unfortunately, we didn't follow through on the idea. I'm convinced that line of the business would have been worth hundreds of millions of dollars to Fmali.

Another Market Finders short-lived consulting client was Westbrae Foods near Berkeley, California, with a big line of healthy foods. The company had a number of investors, many of them family, including the key person who I got along with very well. One of the non-family investors, a man from England, accompanied me to a meeting with a potential client, a large tourist attraction supplying food to its guests.

We had a breakfast meeting scheduled, and just as I was ready to go downstairs, I received a call from Birkum Cheese, my client from Denmark. It was important enough that I couldn't get off the call for 25 minutes. That made me 30 minutes late to the meeting.

Not acceptable. Our potential client was furious, and Westbrae fired me.

LL: If you're going to be late, take the time to notify the person.

I should have told the Danish company, "I'll call you right back. Let me just get my house in order." Or, I should have arranged to speak to my Danish client later. You can't just be late. If you start compromising on your decisions, it can hurt you a lot.

Market Finders was a business-to-business sales and marketing company that reinforced for me the fact that in business, relationships matter. I was a national sales agent for Birkum Cheese, and our main item was cheese sticks that we sold to Slim Jim, with whom I had just started developing a business relationship.

More than just working as an agent for the cheese sticks, I also helped develop products, concepts, and marketing plans. I'd left Standard Brands in December 1977, then started talking to Slim Jim, and set up a meeting with them in Raleigh, North Carolina, in January, shortly after opening my businesses. This was a crucially important meeting that would set the tone for our relationship.

My flight was scheduled to leave from LaGuardia in New York at 9:35 a.m. on Monday morning. But it snowed over the weekend. They plowed the roads, but instead of three lanes, most of the road had been reduced to only two. The traffic was pretty much at a standstill, and the plane left without me.

No! This is my first relationship-building opportunity with my customer!

What to do? I managed to book a 12:35 flight out of Newark, a 40-minute drive, except that the traffic was impossible in that direction, too. By 11:15 a.m., totally stuck and going nowhere, I was close to panicking. In desperation, I drove onto the shoulder, slammed my foot on the gas, and plowed through, arriving at Newark airport just in time. I parked the car and flew to the ticket counter.

"The flight has been delayed for one hour," the ticket agent said.

The air whooshed out of me like a pricked balloon.

But I got there. The Slim Jim folks were delighted to see me, and we had a successful meeting.

LL: It's amazing what we'll do as entrepreneurs to create and sustain our businesses. As an entrepreneur, you have a lot of passion for what you do.

You're the one who turns the lights on in the morning and off at the end of the day. It's all up to you.

Mr. Albertus, the owner of Birkum Cheese, would travel to the United States for about three weeks each year. A lot of his business was with the gift-packing trade. During the Christmas season, cheese was a popular item in gift baskets. Birkum made processed triangles and squares in different flavours, wrapped appropriately for the season. Mr. Albertus would sit in a meeting and say, "I'm not leaving this room until I get an order."

And he did get the order. Every time. He had his own way of motivating sales.

We were doing well, but there was an issue with the cheese sticks that we were selling to Slim Jim, to the tune of millions of dollars. At the end of the cheese stick tubes, where the machine cut them off, a residual piece was left over that would mold. Eventually, because we couldn't figure out how to solve the issue, we had to disband the line.

Through Slim Jim, we were presented with a tremendous opportunity to sell millions of dollars of cheese wedges to Eastern Airlines. The wedges would be paired with crackers as a snack on their flights, a replacement for the pretzels they were currently serving.

The meeting was set up, and we were assured it was going to be a slam-dunk. We arrived: Mr. Albertus, a representative from Slim Jim, a salesman, and I, ready to write the order.

We walked into the buyer's office, who said, "What are you doing here?"

"We were told you were looking for cheese wedges," I said.

"No, I'm not," he countered. "I'm very happy with my pretzels, and they're a lot cheaper."

We were stunned.

LL: But at least I learned something: don't count your chickens before they've hatched. And also, if it sounds too good to be true, it probably isn't true. I've had to learn that many times.

CHAPTER 10

Food Brokerage, Important Lessons, and Perseverance

In addition to doing these two consulting jobs, I was also buying and selling cheese, a form of arbitrage, while also establishing a sales agency, working hard, and juggling a lot of hats at once. All my relationships were BtoB. Essentially, I was a middle person, and cultivating strong relationships was essential. I was looking for ways to improve the product, the delivery, and the relationships. My wife and I were adding value to the product when it passed through our hands. Bottom line: we were the added value because we put our knowledge, care, enthusiasm, and creativity into everything we did.

Our business grew rapidly, and as it did, we found key suppliers, mainly in cheese, that we sold between Baltimore and Boston. In time, we added turkey, ham, roast beef, frankfurters, and other items for the deli cases of the supermarkets and retail delis. We also sold to distributors in the provisions trade. We hired five salespeople, paying them fifty percent of our commission. Some were making as much as $200,000 in 1978, and they were extremely happy.

Twice, we took our key people and customers to Atlantic City for the weekend, making them feel appreciated and important.

LL: I'd already learned that people needed to feel they mattered. People get lonely, and it's valuable for them to be in a venue where they can meet their peers.

I was the front guy in our business. My wife handled the salesmen, needy customers, and the suppliers on day-to-day issues. I was too impatient and results-oriented, so I went on key sales calls and visited the suppliers. One time, we attended a big dinner for a couple of hundred key distributors, and we were the honored guests. I think it was because, despite our degrees, we were down-to-earth, honest, and authentic with everyone.

I had excellent macro-knowledge in economics. I could be totally hands-on, and I could move up and down any level of communication and interaction that was necessary. I understood research from my experience in acquisitions. Everything I'd learned in school and in my work experiences helped me create a thriving business.

LL: We were also transparent in all our dealings. Our suppliers and customers appreciated that. They weren't college-educated elites, but they understood the value of hard work, frankness, and honesty.

Market Cheese Traders purchased off-market cheese, up to hundreds of thousands of pounds at a time, and then located customers who wanted to buy it. The suppliers might sell it for 60 cents a pound to us, and we might sell it for 75 cents to our customers. We had the information that the seller did not as to who wanted the product. Just like oil, cheese has different grades and forms, and is needed in different locations. We had all that valuable information. We found niches of need and put those niches together with customers who had what that market needed.

LL: The one who has information is king.

We also hired a couple of key managers for the business who developed relationships with both the suppliers and the customers.

The relationships we built were essential, but also critical to our success was keeping track of our numbers. Every week, I received a summary of our profit and loss for the period. It wasn't perfectly detailed, but it kept me informed in real time of where we were.

Some people worry that some of the numbers don't come in on time every week. That's not an issue because you can make reasonable assumptions based on past performance, and any missing numbers carry over to the next week.

If you don't get fast, reliable numbers, you may miss a crucial item. You may be in a current situation that you don't discover until six weeks pass. It's so much better to know about it immediately. You may assume that when something goes wrong and no one refers back to it, it's handled.

It isn't handled until it gets handled. Situations don't "just resolve themselves." If you have immediate numbers, you can take care of issues right away. And your numbers don't have to be only dollars and cents. You may want to know about customer calls, quality issues, productivity, or volume. You decide on which quick numbers you need for your business that let you know how well you are doing.

It doesn't matter what line of work you're in—this is useful advice.

If you can't do it because you don't have the time or you just don't want to, it pays to have someone do that for you. I personally like going over the numbers each week. I find it immensely satisfying. It's tangible proof that we're going in a good direction, and, quite frankly, that's very fulfilling. It may not be person-to-person feedback, but it's still a direct response to what I'm doing, and that's incredibly valuable.

LL: No matter what business you're in, I'd advise you to develop an information set that can be put together quickly in a

timely manner, and then use it consistently to evaluate your returns.

One of our key salesmen stole a major provisions supplier and went off on his own. The supplier had been paying us several hundred thousand dollars per year in commissions, so we felt the loss. I could understand why the supplier went with our salesman. At the time, we were developing a new business, Alpine Lace Cheese, and the supplier was concerned we would lose interest in them. That would never have happened, but I could understand their point of view. Still, I was angry. We had tripled an already large business over five years.

We were upset when our salesman left, but we also benefited. We'd lost money, but that loss pushed us to develop our Alpine Lace business.

LL: I've found that many times, when you have a problem and you dig in and solve it, you end up with a satisfying result. I tend to do well when I have a problem to deal with.

We spent more time on our other lines of business, and eventually, our new product line, Alpine Lace, became very large and valuable indeed.

I also learned about the price of loyalty. As an entrepreneur, I tended to have a strong sense of loyalty to people I worked with and people who worked for me. There were times I hung on to them too long. I belonged to TAG, a global entrepreneurs' peer group with meetings once a month. One day, they brought in a guest speaker, an entrepreneur, who said a few words that have stuck with me:

LL: "Slow to hire; fast to fire."

Too many entrepreneurs don't follow that advice. They're too loyal. Over the years, that loyalty has been my bane—as you will see.

CHAPTER 11

Family

My daughter, Karen, was seven when we started Market Finders, our brokerage business and cheese trading company. We were far from rich. Our office was a small room in our house, and we didn't even have a separate telephone line. We just picked up our old black rotary-dial phone when it rang, and answered, "Market Finders."

One day, my wife picked up the phone and answered, "Mommy Finders."

Oops!

And then there was the day my daughter answered the phone very professionally. "Hello. Market Finders."

When I got on the phone with my supplier, he said, "It was really nice talking to your secretary."

Well then!

I learned something when I went out on my own. When I was still with Brooke Bond Foods, I'd had a large customer in Los Angeles named Mo, who bought a lot of products from us. Mo loved me. He'd even met my family when we took a trip to the West Coast. The mutual affection flowed all around.

And then I went into business for myself and went to see Mo. He blew me off. However, other friends I wasn't counting on came through for me.

LL: If you're at a crossroads in your life, you don't really know what will happen next. The best you can do is move on. I was okay, but I learned then that you can't always count on the people you thought you could.

My Danish counterpart at Birkum Cheese was Preben Tobiassen, an incredibly nice, charming, and delightful man who spoke excellent English. People simply gravitated toward him, and we quickly became good friends.

Our family met him while visiting Denmark on a trip that included Tivoli Gardens Park, an ancient village on an island, the beach, and other wonderful spots. He also visited and stayed at our summer vacation house. He was an optimistic person, which was a great gift to have in life, but all was not perfect.

Later in life, after Mr. Albertus died, Preben started his own cheese business and ended up in jail for mislabelling his product. But it was a Danish jail with a couch, a TV, a phone, and probably very kind guards.

The real punishment was being broke when he was released. I helped him out, and in about 2018, I flew to Denmark to visit him and his wife. His limp was one of the first things I noticed. When I asked, he explained he'd had a stroke.

He had a profound effect on me. Looking at him, knowing what a vital person he was, and knowing some of that vitality had disappeared, genuinely touched me. But he was still happy and still charming, and we picked our friendship up as though we had never been apart.

LL: If you have the gift of being a happy person, it is rare; cherish it.

My wife Marion, our daughter Karen, and I thoroughly enjoyed our vacations every summer. We visited Italy, Las Vegas, France, and many other places. Those times together yielded many wonderful memories, including at least one or two that were remarkable simply because they were anything but typical.

It was the weekend after Labor Day, and Karen was going back to college on Monday. We were in Boulder, Colorado, on Saturday, sweltering in 95°F temperatures. So, we decided to drive up Pike's Peak, where we were told the thermometer was reading 33°F at the top. The drive up would take two and a half hours, and rightly so. The road was steep and winding, and the going was slow. I had a coupon for six donuts at the very top, and I was determined to cash it in.

About 30 minutes from the top, we pulled in at a rest stop with a restaurant. Inside, we saw a sign warning us to watch for vapor lock, which occurs when liquid fuel transforms into vapor while still within the fuel delivery system of a gasoline-fueled engine, disrupting fuel flow and potentially causing stalling or difficulty restarting. This could happen while struggling at high altitudes with an overheating engine.

We got back in the car and kept driving as the road switched harder, tighter, and higher. It also became almost dangerously narrow with no guardrails on the steep drop-offs. Apparently, bicyclists would leave the top early in the morning to cruise down, with a couple of deaths reported every year.

I felt the knot in my stomach as I drove up cautiously. About 500 feet from the top, the car stalled. Beads of sweat were starting to roll down my forehead. Karen was screaming in the back seat, "We're gonna die! We're gonna die!"

She's probably right!

"Shut up, Karen!" I yelled, smacking her leg out of sheer panic.

Karen shut up. Marion pulled the manual out of the glove compartment of our rental car and flipped to the section on vapor lock. There actually was an explanation of vapor lock, probably because it was a common enough occurrence in the state.

As advised, I opened the hood, pumped the gas, and the car started. Good, because we were stranded in the middle of the road and a sizeable lineup had formed behind us.

Fifty feet farther up the road was a pullout. I pulled over, waited for the line of cars to pass us, and turned around. We were not going to make it to the top. I was still sweating. And no donuts.

The next day, it snowed, and by the time we got to the Denver airport, four inches had accumulated on the ground.

That was a memory engraved on all our minds.

LL: Nature can sometimes be in control. Never forget this.

More "interesting" memories were more business-oriented. The Fmali company had customers in what, back then, was called the Brooklyn ghetto. My occasional task was to collect money from them— about $300 each time. I'd park the car near the store, and hope it would still be there when I got back. I'd also hope that I'd actually get back.

Meanwhile, in our brokerage business, we had a customer in Connecticut who was delinquent with payments to our cheese suppliers, so my wife drove up there. A lot of our customers were Italian cheese distributors who, I suspect, had "connections" at some point but had found legitimate business a safer and more profitable enterprise.

Marion picked up a check from the supplier because we didn't trust them to mail it. When she got back, she told me that when she walked in, the customer had a gun in a holster on his belt. She got the check, but she was shaking with fear.

Marion always had a wonderful vocabulary. She loved language and knew how to use words. However, the people we dealt with in our brokerage business were street savvy more than book smart. Marion learned to talk their language, to the temporary detriment of her own vocabulary. But those people had a moral compass. They worked hard, and so did their customers.

My admiration for them grew as I got to know them. More than once, in 1978, I spent a week on the delivery truck with Slim Jim, visiting the bars, bodegas, and delis that stocked our cheese sticks. I learned to appreciate the hard-working shopkeepers and delivery drivers. I originally just wanted to see how our cheese sticks were received and how they were marketed at the retail level, but along the way, I got a broader education about how America worked and what was going on in our world.

LL: My wife and I got to meet and know people from all walks of life, and came to understand the value of trust, honesty, and openness. What a valuable lesson!

CHAPTER 12

Developing Alpine Lace

Marion and I were operating a robust food brokerage business as well as a successful cheese trading company when we were inspired to develop a reduced-fat, reduced-sodium, reduced-cholesterol cheddar cheese that we called Premonde, meaning "first world." The idea was to trade in on the panache of European brands, like Häagen-Dazs had with its distinctly European-inspired name, even though it was made in the United States.

We contacted a source in Wisconsin to develop the cheese and again, used BtoB advertising, specifically in *The Cheese Reporter*, a trade newspaper with a circulation between 5,000 and 10,000. We bought a big double-page spread, illustrating a major city skyline, and stating, "Introducing Premonde Cheese!", going for the impression that our cheese was going to take the world by storm.

We also hired a public relations agency, whose campaign involved our appearance at movie premiers, museum and gallery openings, and other gala events. Our agent's husband was involved in the movie business, and we managed to get excellent celebrity endorsements at premieres where our cheese was served. Robert Redford ate our cheese at one opening night, and Billy Joel snacked on it at a museum event. That allowed our agency to write a piece that included a quote from Robert Redford and others. The general feeling was that we were knowledgeable, important, and popular.

Our Premonde was distributed to specialty retail cheese shops and supermarket sections of grocery stores, and became nicely profitable, topping out at about $1.5 million in sales within two years. At that point, our momentum came to a screeching halt, and it happened like this:

Art Coffin, a friend who had worked for me at Brooke Bond Foods, had a brainstorming session with us, telling us, "You're wasting your time on cheddar cheese. The cheese that is much more popular in the reduced-sodium, reduced-fat market is Swiss cheese."

Eureka!

It sounded like excellent advice. We found a source and immediately started developing a Swiss cheese that we intended to call Premonde Swiss. However, we first did a focus group, consisting mostly of women, who told us they hated the name, Premonde, which some associated with premenstrual. End of Premonde. So, we hired an advertising agency, which came up with a hundred other names. We chose to go with Alpine Lace Swiss.

LL: When you bring a group in to help you brainstorm and think, you come up with alternative approaches you may not have thought about. A lot of people could get stuck thinking, "No. This is my idea! My company!" That attitude is not necessarily helpful. You're better off expanding your horizons and being open to new ideas.

Alpine Lace still sounded European, but we were making the point that Alpine Lace Swiss was a high-quality product. The bonus was reduced fat and reduced sodium. It worked. We got the distribution we needed and then embarked on our first advertising campaign.

Being a person who likes to keep a close eye on the budget and doesn't like to risk money I can't afford to lose, I went low-budget. We put together an ad that featured cheesy wedge-shaped hats and actors dressed like a cat and a mouse wearing the hats. I'm pretty sure it went down in advertising history as one of the worst ads ever created.

Meanwhile, Marion and I attended a wedding in Montreal, Canada, for a person who worked for us and was marrying a socialite. Sitting at our table were a wealthy couple from Mississippi: Dudley Hughes and his wife. They took an immediate liking to us, especially to Marion. At one point that evening, Dudley said, "I want to invest in your business."

It wasn't just the champagne talking. He invested about $700,000, giving him 15% of the company, and allowing us to take out $350,000 for ourselves. That in itself was extremely rare. New investors generally want their funds to go solely into the company.

LL: Go with luck. Or was it genius? Dudley and his wife made 2,000% on their investment.

It turned out that Dudley's daughter was married to a man with marketing experience, so we sat down with him and showed him our "cheese hat" ad. He was polite, telling us it was awful in the most tactful way possible. The good news was that it never saw the light of day.

LL: As an entrepreneur, you make a lot of mistakes. The idea is to work your way through them and hopefully learn from them. Most importantly, you need to have people around you who will be honest with you. Probably 70% of entrepreneurs make mistakes. The successful ones are either carried by the marketplace because their idea is that good, or they correct their mistakes. You have to keep that in mind.

Even the richest man on earth, Elon Musk, admits that he made a lot of mistakes early in his career. He became successful because he corrected them as they occurred. (Some believe that Elon has lost that trait in recent years.)

As a side note, I recently read an article about Roger Federer's greatest commencement address. In it, he states that while he won nearly

80% of his singles matches, his career success rate on points was only 54%. So, when he loses a point, he doesn't dwell on losses, but fully commits to the next point with intensity and focus. Good lesson.

LL: Don't look back. You're not going in that direction.

CHAPTER 13

Alpine Lace Evolves

We started getting more distribution for our Alpine Lace and hired a new advertising agency, operated by Vito Catellano, who was very bright. He and his daughter were basically a two-person show. He, his daughter, Marion, and I came up with our new advertising campaign, involving a good-looking guy (basically, a hunk) in a tank top, whose memorable line was, "I want to take care of myself now, not when I'm fifty."

And then he tucked into a piece of cheese in the style of a young and sexy Albert Finney in the old movie, *Tom Jones.* At the end of the ad, we said, "Alpine Lace: 99.9% cholesterol free; 99.8% percent sodium free."

The facts were true, but what we didn't say was that regular cheese was 99.8 percent cholesterol-free and 99.7 percent sodium-free. I had some qualms about our "honest" claim, but Marion said, "Go with it. We're telling the truth."

It turned out we had a good ad. We had a hunk who got the viewer's attention, and we had a strong nutritional claim. We also had a good team on this, and I was still the front person, while Marion was the rock.

LL: Listen to your advisor or second-in-command.

Alpine Lace Swiss was sold in the deli section of supermarkets, a department that was relatively unbranded. At the time, grocery stores were just beginning to change over to UPC codes for their products. When our product arrived at the checkout, it was entered as "deli," not

Alpine Lace. The only branding we had was on the label on the big blocks of cheese in the deli counter. If we wanted to up our sales, we needed consumers to ask for Alpine Lace by name.

So, we started doing television advertising in local markets, but we did it at a bargain price by finding an agency that specialized in selling remnant space, airtime that was left over—probably because it wasn't prime time—and sold usually 60% cheaper.

The conventional wisdom was to advertise to young people so they would become lifelong users. The remnant space was often in programs targeted to older audiences. We didn't care. We just wanted people to see our ads.

I also learned that people had to see your ad about 12 times in order for it to be effective. Our first market buy was in Cleveland. It worked. People started asking for Alpine Lace at the deli counters. We expanded our advertising to more markets, particularly focusing on the time between January and April when people tended to be on diets after the holidays or preparing for swimsuit season.

We grew new markets at the same time that another company, Boar's Head, a popular upscale deli meat, was approaching expansion using very similar methods to ours. They had a bigger budget and a bigger business, but it was the same idea. We never collaborated with them; we just stumbled on the same bright idea at the same time.

I initiated some unusual marketing activities for Alpine Lace that proved useful and beneficial. In 1990, we developed good relationships with the distributors. We'd already learned what working Americans were looking for in their products, and we could relate.

New York City boasts thousands of delis, bodegas, and small restaurants that sell cheese, mainly for sandwiches. When we operated as a food broker, that trade was important to our business. We had about

25 distributors selling to the truck drivers who delivered to the stores. We decided to ramp things up.

One distributor in particular, M&V, was located several blocks from the Boar's Head main plant, the key distributor east of Chicago of high-quality deli meats. The truck drivers would arrive at Boar's Head at three or four a.m. to pick up various meats, stopping at M&V immediately afterwards to pick up cheese and other grocery items. Boar's Head and M&V together accounted for over 500 truck drivers making their rounds one to three days a week.

Tony Ciuffo, M&V's owner, displayed a unique combination of college education and street smarts. Tony was a big supporter, buying a lot of Alpine Lace, which inspired us to develop marketing programs. Working with him reinforced once again the importance of selling BtoB.

We put on a few contests, the most successful of which involved a fish tank. We set up a number of obstacles in the water. When a contestant dropped a quarter into the tank, the idea was to have it navigate the obstructions to land on a certain spot on the bottom. If it did, the contestant won ten dollars.

For every ten-pound case of cheese a truck driver bought, he would get a dollar in quarters. The guys lined up to play the game. I don't think it was the dollars that were the big incentive. It was the fun of the game and the thrill of winning. None of the guys played with their own quarters; they all bought the cases of cheese, and we sold thousands of cases of Alpine Lace.

LL: Try unconventional forms of marketing to stand out.

Once a year, M&V hosted a dinner dance honoring the truck drivers, and one year, my wife and I were the honored guests. It was a touching tribute to our hard work and relationship with the trade.

Tony was astute, but often slow in paying us, so our salespeople were constantly hounding him for money. Why so slow?

"Well," he told us one time, "I can't pay you because the bookkeeper had a nervous breakdown." I'm pretty sure there was no truth in that, but we did eventually get paid. Tony was doing what entrepreneurs do, figure out how to make it work. I admire that.

We did a lot of business with Tony; about $3 to $4 million in sales, but there was no reason it couldn't get bigger yet. We went on Sirius radio with the broadcaster jock, Howard Stern. He turned out to be an astute businessman, understanding our concept immediately. He and his assistant, Robin, went over our material, got it, and in 25 minutes had our marketing idea down pat.

They promoted our cheese, and again, it was a clever BtoB marketing ploy. The truck drivers listened to Howard Stern, and we were focused on building our trade, not so much with the consumer, but with the guys who brought our product to them. We also ran a contest for the distributors. When they sold a case of Alpine Lace, they got a tear-off coupon, entering them into a grand draw for a Mazda Miata, valued at $20,000.

Ultimately, we had a big party and a drawing at our home. To our chagrin, the winner happened to be M&V's much smaller competitor across the street. Our marketing campaigns were very successful. We grew our business to about $10 million per year, and yes, we spent money, but we got a great return.

We also built our reputation for honesty and fairness, a code of trust. If we'd stepped on toes or done anything wrong, we'd have been in trouble. Trust was everything with our distributors.

LL: If you understand what drives middle America, you're a step ahead in marketing your products. In today's world, you have to understand people who use TikTok and other social media platforms.

In our day, we chose to go, not to the ultimate consumer, but to the distributor who brought the product to the consumer.

We continued to grow our business, hiring more people, and then, about two years later, supplementing our consumer advertising with coupons. By that time, individual deli items in the supermarkets had separate codes. The coupons encouraged people to go to the deli to buy our product. Alpine Lace was a good-quality product we obtained from a key supplier in Wisconsin, a family business consisting of the father, two sons, and the wife of one of the sons.

The father, his two sons and his wife, and I developed an excellent relationship. He invested considerably in their plant, laying down about 20 miles of piping. They grew a very large business selling us cheese under our label. It was a solid partnership that continued after the father passed away. In fact, the kids and their wives even attended our daughter's wedding.

By 1993, Alpine Lace had evolved into national advertising. Once again, we bought remnant space, averaging an 80% discount. Generally, good space was available on the Sunday night movie slots once a month because they were highly rated for viewership, but shunned by regular advertisers because the films were considered racy in those days.

It worked well. I can't credit my own genius for that. It was our agency that led us to the remnant space seller. But we were willing to try new things. Sometimes they work and sometimes they don't, but I think you have to be open to trying.

LL: Be willing to try new things.

CHAPTER 14

The Further Development of Alpine Lace

For several years, we sold Alpine Lace cheese to the specialty and delicatessen distribution trade, chalking up modest sales with fairly good distribution. But at that point, I stopped. I needed more information to understand how to market to consumers. I interviewed five or six advertising agencies, several market research firms, and a few consultants, coming away with knowledge I hadn't had. With each interview, I learned about new strategies, including media buying.

LL: Stop periodically; it's a good idea to pause and take on a learning experience. For me, it was an amazing step forward.

We also learned about the importance of trade relationships. Our key consultant was Jay Sheloff, who came with us to a big sales meeting in Colorado, where we conducted a brainstorming session with our brokers. Jay was a dynamic guy who wore a wooden leg that he liked to knock on from time to time, and he had sharp insights. At the meeting, he pointed out the significance of trade relations by asking, "In the distribution chain, who is the most valuable link?"

Good question! We pondered it. Well, the deli clerks behind the counter who sliced the cheese. As with most everything, loyal customers made up over 50% of the supermarket deli business. They would come into the store several times a week and would get to know the deli clerks. In other words, the clerks were our emissaries. Our job was to make them our spokespeople or ambassadors.

At that time, we hired Bill Helmreich, another marketing consultant who did a different kind of research for us. He visited various delis, saying his wife had asked him to buy a nutritional cheese and asked the clerk what made Alpine Lace so special. Most flunked the test. So, with the information that our most important link didn't know us and our virtues, we developed a unique marketing plan.

Our system consisted of about seventy local sales agency brokerages with about 15 people in each, giving us a force of about 1,000 people. They went out to the deli clerks, asking them to fill out a simple form, reinforcing that our cheese was lower in fat, sodium, and calories, and that our product quality was higher than our major competitor, Lorraine Cheese, doing about 25% less business than us. However, Lorraine was lower-priced and, as a result, it was keeping a lid on our pricing.

So, we created the questionnaires, gave the clerks a short tutorial, and presented them with a free, fun-looking T-shirt or a red Alpine Lace hat. From that point, we soared past Lorraine, even though we were higher-priced. We even managed to raise our margins to seventy cents higher than Lorraine's.

I actually met Lorraine's CEO on a flight one time. He wanted to know how we were doing so well. Naturally, I didn't tell him our secrets, but he also implied he would raise his prices. I said, "Fine." I wasn't about to get into price fixing.

He never did raise his prices.

LL: We were exploring and learning that outside catalysts can really help open your eyes.

The International Deli Dairy Bakery Association trade show was another key component in our success. Almost all the major supermarket buyers attended. Like the deli clerks, the buyers were crucial to our success. No matter how good your advertising is, if your product isn't merchandised correctly, it won't do as well as it should.

The whole point was to get the supermarkets to feature and display our products more than the competition's, or in fact, any cheese or deli meat. Naturally, the key sales agent in each market was critical to our relationship with the supermarket chains. If our sales agents weren't engaged with us or the supermarket buyers, it wouldn't go well for us. Each agent might represent 30 lines in the deli, and they had to decide who they were going to feature in the big Easter or July 4 ads, for example. The supermarket might give the agent two items in the ad, and obviously, we wanted to be one of the two.

To enhance good trade relationships, we attended the big annual trade show attended by our agents and the supermarket buyers. One year, Jordan Greenberg, our head of marketing, came up with the idea of hiring the baseball player, Pete Rose. At the time, he was living down his prior trouble due to a betting scandal. He was also known for having a short, nasty temper, but he was famous.

On the Friday before the trade show began, he played golf with about 30 of our key supermarket buyers and brokers. On Saturday, he attended the show, signing baseball gloves, bats, trading cards, baseballs, and hats. The attention he received was almost overwhelming. Bringing him to the show cost us $25,000. One supermarket buyer wanted a baseball glove, bat, and ball for his kids. In gratitude, he gave us $25,000 worth of free ads.

A coup! And one of the best investments we ever made.

LL: Think outside the box.

After that, we hired Kim Alexis, a Sports Illustrated swimsuit model, married at that time to the hockey star, Ron Duguay. She was our spokesperson, appeared at trade shows, and helped us a good deal. However, two years later, when she chose to do a Monistat ad for yeast infections, we broke off the relationship. We felt a yeast infection medication would never be compatible with cheese.

We continued to be innovative in our promotions. In 1988, we were able to get the rights from the International Olympic Committee for $50,000 to make an Olympic cheese. We called it Olympiad—a cheddar cheese with extra nutritional virtues. But we made a few compromises along the way, and it failed.

The five Olympic rings were on the packaging. It tasted okay. Not great, but certainly not bad. However, we ended up with only a fair product and we never marketed it properly, just assuming it would fly off the shelves.

LL: In life, when you start compromising, even little compromises, especially if you compromise your values, you're going to fail.

We took our loss on Olympiad. Still, it was a brilliant idea, and we had a ten-year contract! You never know. Look at Oprah. In 2017, she debuted her food line in collaboration with Kraft Heinz, called *O, That's Good!* It included potato products like mashed potatoes and baked potato soup, and it flopped. Just because someone's name is on the product doesn't mean it's going to be successful.

Doctor Cheddar was another amazing flop. Sid Caesar was the star of *Your Show of Shows* with his wife, Imogene Coca, which ran from 1950-1954. He was an amazing slapstick comedian who played a variety of characters, including a nutty doctor. At one point, he had drug problems, kicked them, and made a comeback. At Alpine Lace Brands, we developed an imitation cheese with no cholesterol made out of vegetable oils, called Doctor Cheddar, and we tapped Sid Caesar as our spokesperson (Doctor Cheddar), hiring him to do a television ad, and feeling certain our older customers would know and like him. At the time, he was starring in a show at The Village Gate in New York City. The agent set up a meeting at his hotel. Sid said he wanted $200,000 for his endorsement. The agent, my marketing guy, and I went back downstairs. "There's no way we're going to pay him that," I said to the agent. "We'll give him $15,000."

The agent went back upstairs, came down, and said, "We'll take it."

LL: You never know if you don't try.

To continue this story, Sid Caesar was a health nut, demanding precise kinds of foods from very exact suppliers. And then he took it a step further, telling us what we should eat, too.

We filmed the commercial, making sure he had what he wanted on set. My marketing guy told me that after they wrapped the shoot, they went to dinner at a restaurant in Little Italy where Sid Caesar "ate everything that walked."

The ad did help Doctor Cheddar's sales, but the product was before its time. Honestly, it also wasn't all that great. We should have cancelled it. Instead, we compromised.

LL: Same mistake. Don't compromise.

During the last four years that we owned Alpine Lace, we created major events for our sales agents and some supermarket buyers, taking them on cruises or to the Four Seasons on Maui.

The brokers who came with us were the winners of contests. Each one had to meet a quota between September and December, traditionally our slowest months, because grocery stores were promoting regular and holiday food rather than nutritional products. Our brokers had to convince the supermarket buyers to promote our products. If they agreed and merchandized us heavily, we would sell four or five times more than we otherwise would.

Each year, we raised the bar for the quota. The last trip to Hawaii included about 100 people and cost us about $150,000 all in. It was so worth it. Our sales increased by $10 million at that difficult time of year and brought in about $2 million in incremental profits.

LL: One of the first lessons I mentioned holds true: people want to feel important.

The brokers loved the trips. They could meet with their peers, and they were treated well. On each trip, we spent only a modest amount of time on business. The majority of the time was all about leisure and fun.

Because of the missed opportunity of bottled tea with Fmali, I looked into snack distribution with Alpine Lace, but determined it didn't make sense. Why would a company known for nutritional cheese be going into the snack business? To this day, I think it was a big marketing mistake.

If you have a product that has virtues and is selling well, you can gain distribution by giving away product, because, ultimately, you are going to get the sales. This is part of a concept called *lifetime marketing value.* The idea behind lifetime marketing value is that the upfront costs of procuring a customer are worth it many times over for the value of having the customer return for many years.

With a product like beverages or snacks, the upfront costs are low compared to the probability of garnering sustained sales over a long period of time. Many products have done extremely well in the long term due to their natural virtues. The latest of these is Celsius, an energy drink containing natural fruit flavors with no artificial preservatives or flavors, no aspartame or high fructose corn syrup, and a very low sodium content.

Virtue products are easy to identify in the liquor business with vodka, Scotch, and premium wines. In convenience stores and supermarkets, you see it with juices and sparkling water brands. Remembering that there are several hundred thousand distribution points for snack and beverage products, there's a huge market. A snack product would start out in a small independent corner store or deli. My experience selling cheese sticks with Birkum cheese (Slim Jim) told me that you could incentivize the drivers of the trucks, the main link in your distribution channels, to feature your products with bonuses and other rewards.

LL: The key to success in all this is that the product has to have a natural appeal with sustainable, good quality virtues, and you have to know how to get it through the distribution channels.

LL: If you find a business opportunity where your model shows limited risk and great reward, you should really go for it.

There are many snack companies that have been sold for hundreds of millions of dollars. Nabisco acquired Tate's Cookies, a delicious wafer-thin cookie, several years ago after it had grown into a modest-sized company based on its quality and concept.

But now we were getting back to reality, and our time with Alpine Lace wasn't all smooth sailing. We had plenty of challenges and obstacles to get through.

CHAPTER 15

Mountain Farms

In the early 1990s, we bought Mountain Farms, a company located in Logan, Utah, supplying packaged cheeses to supermarket chains, and doing about $30 million in annual sales. They bought large blocks of cheese, cutting it into consumer chunks, or slicing it or shredding it, and selling it to supermarkets.

We also bought Marolf Farms, a cheese company in South Dakota selling quality cheddar cheese, Colby, and Monterey Jack in eight-ounce half-moon retail packs, mainly to the West Coast. It was a much smaller company, doing around $2 million in business annually. It didn't cost much, and we simply absorbed it.

We ran into serious trouble with Mountain Farms. The company made a profit of about $500,000–$700,000 annually. We purchased it for two or three million. It wasn't an exciting company, but it brought in a steady profit and added to our return while increasing our sales. The president of the company, who lived in Salt Lake City, was a capable man who did a good job running the enterprise. He was also excellent at customer relations and had built up a nice business.

In the mid-nineties, our advertising, which had always paid off for us, was not producing the bump in sales we had previously experienced. Our quarter ended in March. In April, we decided to write off the year and take our loss. At that time, we were also changing banks, and simply wrote off the advertising.

A few months later, in July, my wife and I were in Florida visiting our daughter when I got a call telling me that Mountain Farms was showing a $600,000 loss for the second quarter.

What!?

I was on the phone for two hours trying to figure out what had happened. There was no discernible reason for this. Mountain Farms was a company that reliably did its business and brought in its profits with never an issue. It made no sense. The rest of the week, I spent many hours on the phone in Florida trying to sort it out, but without making progress.

My certified public accountants, one of the larger firms in the country, suggested I go out to Utah, saying I'd probably get a better handle on it if I were there. They also told me not to say anything to the bank until the numbers were definite. On Sunday, I booked a plane ticket to Salt Lake City. My VP of finance chose not to come with me. I flew out on Monday, and called my bank, and frankly said, "I'm on my way out to Utah. We have a sudden $600,000 loss, and we don't know what's wrong."

It wasn't an easy issue to solve. I was in Utah for a month, trying to uncover the facts. The cheese market had been volatile that year. Albertson's, a large grocery chain that was one of Mountain Farms' big customers, had hired a new buyer who immediately took a dislike to Mountain Farms, possibly because he had a friend who was a competitor. We couldn't be sure, but we were afraid he would swing his business over to the friend.

Mountain Farms kept its price down for a couple of months in order to compete sharply, meaning it lost money. All of this occurred in the first and second quarters, but because they always showed a profit, the controller, a CPA, falsified the books for the first quarter, showing a normal $150,000 profit. In fact, they had lost $200,000.

By June, the controller realized he couldn't keep it up. In July, he came clean.

Ultimately, Mountain Farms lost Albertson's, giving up 50 percent of their business. It wasn't my first crisis, and I knew that when you were in that sort of situation, you did what you had to do to sort it out. We tightened up overheads, figured out ways to be more efficient, and managed to get the business back up to breaking even by September.

However, we had to show the loss on our books, which we did, giving a full and accurate explanation to the bank, which was very satisfied with how I'd handled it.

But I was still upset that my CFO had not gone to Utah with me. On top of that, I was told that he'd said to the bank, "You're lucky you have me because Carl likes to push the books."

That was absolutely wrong. Was he trying to make himself look important?

I sat down with the bank in September and said, "I'll be terminating the CFO. He didn't go out to Mountain Farms, and he's just not the right person for the job."

I gave him notice, and he was gone by December. The bank didn't even blink, because they knew I was being honest and open with them.

LL: When you have a loss, you must roll up your sleeves and dig in as the owner/principal. Sometimes you have to go it alone, but in the end, you are the one responsible.

I also terminated the CFO at Mountain Farms, and he left in September. Then I terminated the president of Mountain Farms as of December. He wasn't surprised when I said, "Look, you can't do that. You have to deal with things and come clean. And the fact you didn't means I can't have you here."

Two years later, we sold Mountain Farms to Weston Foods at about break-even. Meanwhile, we converted Marolf Farms into a highly efficient slicing facility for Alpine Lace.

CHAPTER 16

The Challenges of Alpine Lace

N o business has a smooth run all the time, just like no entrepreneur turns every single thing he touches into gold. There will always be times that are tough. However, the hardships we experience often produce their greatest lessons.

In our earlier days, we had a bank loan from a local bank that had a one-man satellite office in our commercial building in New Jersey. We had a $2.5 million loan with them and applied for an additional $2 million for working capital.

Our banker said, "No problem."

The day the loan was supposed to come through? Nothing. "No problem," he said. "We'll just set you up with an overdraft."

We had an overdraft of about $1 million the day I flew to South Dakota and learned that my checks were bouncing. Apparently, our local loan officer had just been caught committing fraudulent activity with a client, and anything he did was suspect.

I had to fly back immediately and figure out how to cover the checks. Meanwhile, the bank's head office lumped me in with the loan officer and said, "We don't trust you. We're calling your loan. In fact, we're going to call it in right away unless you guarantee it with your stock."

We had two lawyers: a general counsel and a Securities and Exchange (SEC) lawyer. The general counsel said, "No problem."

I was scared sh**less, but said okay to the bank, figuring the stock would be worthless if the loan was called. However, I decided to discuss the bank situation at an emergency board meeting a few days later, and our SEC lawyer said, "You can't put up your stocks as security. It's reportable, and your stock will get destroyed. You have to tell him you can't do it, and there are rules that prevent loans from being called suddenly."

I called the bank right in the middle of my board meeting and told them, "I'm not doing it. I'm not guaranteeing it, and you can't call the loan."

They obviously knew all that, because they immediately capitulated and gave me six months to find a new loan, which we were in full compliance with anyway.

We found a new bank shortly afterwards, which later became Bank of America.

LL: Interestingly, both the worst and the best advice can come from professionals. Get a second opinion.

Was I worried about all this? Panicking? What do you think?

LL: I tend to do well in the toughest situations, and I think that's because I focus on options. It's helpful to do that. Don't assume any situation is either/or. Look for your options. You may be surprised how many there are. And yes, I was under considerable stress, but sometimes, when you're stretched thin, you do your best work.

I reverted to doing what I did when we had the bread distribution company. I figured out our cash flow and managed it carefully while negotiating our new bank loan with a larger bank with whom I built a good relationship.

We founded our company in 1983 and went public in 1986 with a small brokerage, Beuret & Company. We were Beuret's first offering.

Going public had been my dream, so I was pretty excited. The brokerage raised about $3 million for us, but all small-cap stocks were not doing well after that.

Beuret was backing a lot of small companies whose stocks were crashing, but he made up his mind to keep up the price of the stocks he had raised capital for, telling his salespeople, "You cannot sell stock of any company that we support." Unwisely, he used his shares of each of the companies he supported as capital, and if the price went down, so did his equity. He would go broke if the shares went down too much.

If someone wanted to sell 1,000 shares of Alpine Lace, Beuret would not execute the order. Of course, because Beuret was good to me, I also owned a good portfolio of his companies, and when I wanted to sell some of my shares, the answer was, "No dice."

I was afraid those companies would collapse, so I moved my stocks to another company and sold them.

LL: There are always options if you look for them.

Beuret finally went out of business and we developed relationships with larger firms. We were doing well enough that we appeared in articles in several magazines as one of the top growing companies in the entire country. We exploded from $6 million in sales to $12 million to $18 million to $45 million to $70 million. We were touted as a dynamic company and capitalized on our new reputation by doing public relations and major events.

Oppenheimer & Company Inc., a multinational financial services company offering investment banking, was one of our key supporters and our investment banker. An analyst followed our progress closely, and as our star continued to rise, we were approached to sell the company. By then, our stock had moved up from a dollar a share to $10.

As word got out that we might sell, both rumors and trading volume increased. The stock went up to $14, and we were short raided (or short seller attacked), meaning a short seller—in our case, The Fishbacks from Texas—was making a concerted effort to drive down the price of our stock by selling borrowed shares with the goal of making our share price fall, allowing them to buy the shares back later at a lower price and profit from the difference.

If we were going to sell our company, and The Fishbacks were shorting our stock, they were going to be stuck. If the company were sold, shareholders would have to turn in their stock. Not only would the stock go up, but it would rise sky high, and the Fishbacks were naturally concerned about a sale. They had to buy the stock back at a cheap price, not at a higher one than they were bargaining for.

So, they started by getting a number of articles written telling the public we were a fly-by-night firm—anything to drive down the price of our stock.

They said our labels were wrong, our quality assurance was bad, and our nutritional claims were false.

I was severely stressed, but this was a battle we had to fight and win. In our small office building, we commandeered everyone's fax machine to reply to our reams of messages. It was chaos.

LL: One of our lawyers gave me an excellent piece of advice: Any telephone calls, any communication—only in writing. Everything is on the record. We followed his advice precisely, and it worked.

In the prior weeks, we had been talking to a Dutch company about a sale, and called a board meeting to discuss it. At that meeting, I mentioned there was no actual definition of low-fat, low-sodium, low-cholesterol cheese. The USDA did not have a definition, and only Wisconsin and New York State were defining it in fairly general terms. Our label descriptions were not yet fully defined by government agencies.

The board said, "Don't worry about it."

By now, I'd heard the words, "Don't worry about it," often enough that it should have caused me to be truly apprehensive.

This time, it was one of the worst pieces of advice I ever got.

LL: "Don't worry about it" means worry about it.

On the following Monday, the short sellers got hold of the person who ran the cheese department of the Wisconsin Department of Agriculture, saying we were selling cheese with a label that had not been approved. He immediately put an embargo on thirty cases (300 pounds) of our Munster cheese. The article in Barron's on Saturday alleged we were a fly-by-night firm with illegal labels, false quality, wrong nutritional reporting, and other negative things. So, by late Monday, the news came out in the Wall Street Journal and on the wire that our cheese was embargoed.

Our stock went down a little, but the key analyst at Oppenheimer was determined to fight the Fishbacks and chose to support our stock. He called his friends who bought our stock, and it held.

Meanwhile, we were in serious talks with the potential Dutch buyers and had invited them and our bankers to lunch at our house on that Monday afternoon, going to considerable trouble to make our already beautiful backyard with its swimming pool and waterfall, sparkle, even bringing in additional pots of plants and flowers.

Since the article in *Barron's* had come out early on the Saturday before the scheduled lunch, we asked our investment banker from Oppenheimer, "Do you think we should tell them about the article and discuss it?"

"No, it'll just blow over," He said. "Don't worry."

Great. One more person telling me not to worry.

Again, bad advice. And greed on my part. The buyers were talking about purchasing my shares at $18–$20 per share, and I wanted that money. At the time, the shares were just hanging in at about $12 each.

Oppenheimer played dumb with the Dutch company about our situation.

By Wednesday of that week, the Dutch buyers heard about it and said, "The deal's off."

The shorts had been successful.

How bad was it? One person who worked in our office heard what was happening and sold her shares, and one of our directors tipped off a friend who sold shares. When I found out, I terminated both the director and the employee.

My next job was to meet with the buyers and tell them what was going on. Marion suggested I wait a couple of days because the stock was gyrating and trading at a very high volume. Okay, I called the meeting for 4 p.m. on Friday after the markets had closed for the week, and we didn't have to report that we had no deal. They explained why they were not going to buy the company, not because of the article, but because there was no definition of nutritional cheese.

Meanwhile, to counter the short raids, we got hold of the Wisconsin Department of Agriculture. They released the Munster cheese they had been holding, saying they had made a terrible mistake. New York State said we were in compliance, and the USDA agreed. We got over the allegations, but the damage had been done.

I didn't go with my gut and tell the potential buyers about the label situation upfront, prior to our Monday lunch. That way, it would be *our problem*, and we could deal with it rather than have them find out about it from external sources. Where I followed the life lesson on the problems in accounting at Mountain Farms, I let this situation rule me instead of the other way around.

LL: Deal with an issue up front and look at your options with your partners instead of hiding it.

Even after we announced we had no deal, our friends at Oppenheimer continued to push our stock to their friends, implying that we might have another buyer, and the price went up to $24 per share.

"Can I sell some shares?" I asked.

"Absolutely not! You're an insider!"

Eventually, everything settled down, and I took some time to reflect. What were the shorts saying that was right? They'd said we were sloppy on quality control, which was true. We also had to get our labels defined, which the government did over the next several months. And we did have to run a better operation. We were so heady with our growth that we never thoroughly tied down our operations.

We spent the next year or two laying down solid groundwork and turning our company into a first-class operation.

LL: Operations is the foundation of your business. Without strong processes and a solid foundation, your business has no value.

Goldman Sachs approached us several months after the short raid in 1989, asking if we wanted to sell the company. If the price was right, of course! So we put together an elaborate proposal that included spending $30 million on marketing. We dealt with Jide Zeitlin, one of the firm's top brilliant bankers.

Then, one of the firm's junior, but extremely capable bankers, worked with us for months on the marketing plan.

But that was 1990, the year the Gulf War started, and with the war, everything stopped. Even though nothing came of it, it was a tremendous marketing exercise, involving a memo of at least 100 pages, outlining how to parlay our $100 million brand into a $500 million label.

LL: The exercise may have been futile in the end, but intellectually and business-wise, I earned several graduate degrees in the process. The lesson is, don't be afraid to go out on a limb and think big.

CHAPTER 17

Paradigm Shift

L: Stop periodically; it's a good idea to stop and take on a learning experience. For me, it was an amazing step forward.

After emerging successfully from our short raid, I paused again. This time, Marion and I re-engineered Alpine Lace after reading a book about Business Process Re-engineering (BPR). We were suitably impressed with the concept.

We learned that BPR is a strategic management approach focused on fundamentally rethinking and redesigning core business processes to achieve significant improvements in performance and efficiency. By critically examining and redesigning business processes, BPR improves efficiency, effectiveness, and performance, and improvements that can impact various aspects of the business, including cost, output, service, speed, and quality.

We found a video on paradigms, which are a set of assumptions, beliefs, and practices that influence how we perceive and interact with reality. Paradigms can be helpful in your day-to-day life, but they can also lock you in, essentially putting blinders on you when you explore. When you need to re-engineer, you have to examine your paradigms and notice that what was true in the past may no longer be true in the present or the future.

We set up a number of meetings with our managers and showed them the short 20-minute video we had watched, as well as an episode of Seinfeld, where everyone was making assumptions that got them into a good deal of trouble. The Seinfeld show was particularly good at eliciting laughs and opening everyone up to examining their own assumptions.

We attacked all our operations, including quality assurance, sales and marketing, and expenses. At the same time, we incentivized our employees with bonuses if they met certain operational targets. One of our goals was to eventually move our accounts receivable from an average of 35 days to 26 days. At that point, we were approaching $70 million in annual sales. In any given month, we did $6 million in sales, so by moving those accounts to 26 days, we'd save $1.5 million in cash.

We also analyzed our trucking efficiency. We hired independent truckers across the country, but we needed to make sure those trucks were full. Once implemented, we lowered our cost by about 1% of sales. Annually, that saved us $350,000.

In our assessments, we discovered that we were spending about $400,000 annually on samples through a network of seventy brokers. We got about six sample requests each day. Every time someone wanted a sample of one of our lines of cheeses, we would go to our central warehouse in Chicago, pack the sample in a Styrofoam case, and send it to the broker by Federal Express. The broker would then place it in his big sample refrigerator.

It was a secretary who alerted us. "Do you know how much money we're spending on samples?" she asked.

We had no idea. After we dived in, we learned that the cost of shipping was the same as the actual samples. We also found that the brokers (our sales agents) ordered about a dozen samples at a time to make sure they had some on hand, and by the time they sent them out several weeks later, they weren't as fresh as they should have been.

We changed the system so that I would have to approve each request. We went from six to three, and instead of shipping them, the local salesperson went to an existing customer distribution center. The broker would then pick up the samples the day before they were due to arrive at the retail location. The samples were now fresh and in good condition. We lowered our sample costs by about 60%, saving several hundred thousand dollars a year.

My wife, Marion, handled quality assurance. Each week, we reviewed all customer complaints, about 18 on average. I shrugged, "Oh well, you're going to get about 18 a week."

Marion said, "No way!"

We started going through them, categorizing them, and understanding what the customers were unhappy about. Number one: We sold a lot of sliced cheese in packages. The Swiss cheese was softer than regular Swiss, and the slices would start to stick together in the package. Solution: We put parchment paper between the slices.

Our complaints went down to about four a week.

Customer deductions really ate into our profits, but they were a big generator of profits for the supermarket chains. Whenever they could, they would deduct something. If we fought back, the deduction was often reversed, and they'd know they'd have to be more careful next time. In one case, we had a customer in the Carolinas for whom deductions were a major source of profits. One of the news channels actually did an exposé on them.

In our case, they said they had product that had gone past its "best by" date, and we were responsible for it, and they should get a credit. We discovered it was a lie.

They countered with, "No, it's true."

"Okay," we said. "We're no longer doing business with you."

A few months later, they came back to us and we made a deal: 3% credit on all sales, but no other deductions. As a result, we saved about 5% on sales.

We managed our inventory so that on Fridays, we had about a quarter-week inventory left. Our product was always fresh. But getting to that stage took some work.

If we had high sales for our Swiss cheese in any given week, we would order more for future sales. The lag time between ordering and delivery was about four–five weeks. However, if we had low sales, we would cut back the orders. Fine for us, but not for the manufacturer and the dairy farmers.

The Swiss cheese plant in Wisconsin was our key manufacturer, supplying us with about 600,000 pounds of cheese a week, or 15 truckloads. He told us our yo-yo ordering system meant that the farmers who supplied him with milk wanted to know how much he would need. One week he'd demand twice as much as during a slow week, and then he'd have to pay extra for the milk or the farmers would have to dump it. They weren't happy.

We said, "Okay. We'll give you the same weekly sales needed for the next six months. You'll give us the same quantity every week." That tactic gave us a 2% discount, which added up to $600,000.

Now we had a lower inventory every Friday, because on the weeks when it was piling up, we'd approach a supermarket chain and say, "You have an order for one trailerload. We need two. You're going to get another trailer next week anyway, so why not buy two now?"

It worked: We got rid of the overloads, and in the weeks when we were short, we cut the trailer loads down to 60%, because we knew they had backup from the week before. It worked beautifully.

In our re-engineering, we looked at everything that walked, talked, and breathed.

We had managers in every department, including one who watched the inventory very well. Each manager had a target, and we gave out bonuses to all of them, including the truck manager and the people in charge of the finances. Typically, the bonus was $60 a week. At that time, in the nineties, that was nice pin money that could add up to $3,000 per year on an average salary of about $30,000.

Our people were happy about it.

We also had a big bulletin board charting our efficiencies and making the goals highly visible.

Before our short raid, we were a pretty good operating company. Afterwards, we became a super operating company, and I was pretty darn proud of what we accomplished.

LL: Periodically, stopping and taking time for a learning experience is extremely valuable. You just have to open your mind and be willing to make a paradigm shift. It's all information and options.

Not everyone was pleased with our re-engineering strategies. One of our large investors insisted we evaluate everyone, including me. So, under duress, we brought in a personnel evaluation consultant.

In retrospect, I'd say the woman who did the job was both cagey and political. She asked questions without responding or giving feedback and was successful at putting everyone on edge. None of the managers was happy, including me. One of our people even had a panic attack. In one of our meetings with some of our bankers, when he stood up to speak, he fell apart, and I had to jump in and take over for him.

My opinion? Outside consultants can be good if they have good motivations. In this case, I'm not sure what she accomplished, if anything. The investor who insisted on bringing her in wasn't totally happy with our company, so who knows what his motivations were.

I believe if I had had more courage at the time, I would have spoken up and said, "This person is not good." But the "money people" wanted it done, so I went along with it. No one was fired. Nothing changed. It was just a distraction.

Not long after that, I replaced the investor with another investor who eventually quadrupled their money, and thanked me for years afterwards for the great investment they had made.

LL: You need to be careful with outsiders: they do not always have your best interests in mind.

Marion and I worked well together, but at times I could be high-strung, impatient, and not consistent. Marion was the steady operator who kept me and the operations in line. During one meeting, I was having an off day and was short-tempered with Marion. After the meeting, she said to me, "If you do that again, I am out of here. If you are having a bad day, go take a walk."

I was speechless, mostly because she was absolutely correct.

LL: Sometimes the best advice is not given with kid gloves. But if you can learn from it, it can be the most valuable.

One lesson well learned is that we never crossed each other in front of our employees and did not curry favor by critiquing our partner or family member. We cut off any path going that way. If an employee had an issue, we suggested they go to their superior. In family businesses, family members are often not as professional toward each other as they should be, and the employees start taking sides. Just remember, family always wins.

LL: If you are in a family business, treat family members with respect and fairness, and do not encourage politicking. It will only lead to major issues later, especially for the employees. This applies to all business relationships.

CHAPTER 18

Fat Free Cheese and Patents

We had a terrific and impressive Board of Directors at Alpine Lace, including some strong marketers, a high level person who had worked for General Foods, another big player who started Perrier, a senior VP who worked at Conagra, the head of accounting from one of the top accounting firms in the country, another person on the consulting side of accounting, a partner at the largest security firm in the country, and a highly knowledgeable banker. My wife, Marion, was also on the board. For our size of company it was of very high quality.

I made better decisions back then than I did later. Why was that? Maybe I was more concerned about failing later in life than I was when I was younger. I may also have been full of confidence, given my track record of heading a high-growth company. We were written about in financial magazines as one of the top 50 or 100 growth companies, and enjoyed a great deal of positive press. That probably made a difference.

In the mid-nineties, with the help of a consultant, we developed a fat-free cheese, a totally innovative product. It was a great idea, but it broke the rule.

LL: The product was okay, but the rule is that if it's okay, it's not okay.

We did it anyway. We made fat-free cream cheese and fat-free cheddar cheese, and American slices, but in terms of flavor, they were not sustainable. This was especially crucial for cream cheese, where the flavor and palatability are key factors for consumers. You could get away with just "okay" with some products, but cream cheese had to be right on the money.

We introduced our fat-free cream cheese with a major public relations push at the terminal for the Staten Island Ferries at the foot of Manhattan, with the Statue of Liberty in the background, staging an event where we would give out 25,000 bagels smeared with fat-free cream cheese to commuters. We were written about in 700 newspapers and publications. The publicity was fantastic, but putting the event together was a monumental undertaking.

We hired people to smear the cream cheese on the bagels, having purchased 25,000 of them from a famous high-quality bagel maker in New York City. One of our hopes was that the excellent bagels would hide the slightly bitter taste of the cream cheese.

We also hired the local high school cafeteria and gym, and another 50 kids to smear the cheese. By 1 p.m. the day before the big event, we realized we had only done 8,000 bagels. We added some crazy incentives and wild cheerleading to the task, and when we got it up to 18,000 bagels by 5 p.m., we were done.

"Okay, this is the best we can do."

The people from our plant in Wisconsin came to New York for the event, as well as my wife and daughter, and Dr. Aly Gamay, the inventor of the fat-free process. We had a major news conference, and a few days later, a lunch for several hundred at the prestigious 21 Club, where we worked with the chef on dishes featuring our cheese. We served fat-free cheese quiche and fat-free cream cheese cake. We got millions of dollars of publicity. A stellar product introduction!

Unfortunately, all our publicity couldn't eliminate the problem that the product was just okay. Our sales were also just okay. We did not hit it out of the park. Despite that, Kraft Foods, Borden's Foods, Conagra, and two others turned their attention to what we were doing.

We had a patent, but we still double-checked our product and everything that went into it. We also got a second opinion. We wanted to make sure our patent was strong.

Our law firm had offices in Washington, D.C. and Pittsburgh, and when Kraft came out with a no-fat cheese, our lawyers informed us we would sue them in Newark, New Jersey, where we had our headquarters. If we took them to court on their home turf of Chicago, the local jury might be more inclined to side with them.

I said, "Why don't we just go see them and say 'You're infringing?' We can negotiate with them."

Our lawyers vetoed me. "No, this is worth millions of dollars to you."

LL: Once again, tread carefully when following legal advice. Watch your every step. Greed got in the way again and again.

Our lawyers were on contingency, and we dove right into a major lawsuit. They spent $8 million in free contingency legal time. Today, it would be triple that. Meanwhile, we spent about $500,000 on second opinions, experts, and photocopies.

We went to trial and lost, but only the first round. The appeals court was our next stop, and that had always been the intention. It was the appeals court that was knowledgeable and would decide the merits of the case. But we wouldn't hear back from them for at least a couple of years.

Meanwhile, Kraft's lawyer, from Kirkland and Ellis, one of the top law firms in the country, approached us. "I don't know why you did this," he said. "We would have settled with you."

Right after that, Kraft sued us for undertaking a frivolous lawsuit. I totally blew my cool. This was contrary to everything I stood for, and exactly what I had wanted to avoid. Kraft accused me of making false statements, which was patently not true. The lawsuit was summarily thrown out.

LL: Avoid lawsuits whenever possible. They can cost more money than they are worth.

CHAPTER 19

The Deal

Meanwhile, our stock price was doing fine; it had come down a bit, but was still trading at $4–$6 a share, but all this lawsuit business was eating up a lot of my attention.

Then, in the late nineties, lower-fat cheese was a trend that was beginning to fade. We were still doing well, but I was a bit concerned that it was time for a change, not even necessarily for Alpine Lace, but for me. I was ready to move on.

I was pretty sure it was time for me to become a Board of Directors superstar. Given what I'd done with Alpine Lace, CEOs of major corporations would be banging down my door.

However, I had some issues to deal with first. Whenever milk prices went up— every third year or so—our margins took a modest hit. If milk prices went up a lot, we took a bigger hit because supermarkets were reluctant to raise prices. On top of that, we were competing with everyone else, so we would be squeezed. If deli meat prices didn't go up, the supermarkets would highlight those items instead of ours. Other cheese companies, particularly if they weren't in the nutritional category, were also likely to hold their prices, especially if they were a co-op with the farmers also making the cheese, as well as supplying the milk. If milk prices were higher, their total margin would actually increase.

The end result was more pressure on us as our margins were squeezed by two or three points, bringing gross profit down to about

22%. Meanwhile, the goal of our business plan was to bring the margins up to the low thirties, giving us a profit of 10%. In a good year at that time, we were making 5–7%. If we hadn't implemented all the efficiencies we had, our profits would have been only 2 or 3%, and that wasn't unusual in our industry.

The plan we had developed with Goldman Sachs was to spend more dollars on marketing. That made sense. If you're a $500 million company and you spend 5% on advertising and marketing, you're paying out $25 million. You'd expect to see an additional $50 million in gross profit and $25 million in profit after paying the $25 million in marketing expenditures. It was a great concept, but it never materialized.

Then Bill Nash came along, one of the best promoters and salesmen I'd ever met. Bill had been my stockbroker and was working at the time for Merrill Lynch. He introduced me to Merrill Lynch's banking department, which made a presentation centered on selling our company.

Our cycles were still going up and down, but the one thing you can't have on Wall Street is a down year. That is, you can be down, just not down in profits. I also had a tendency to over-project profits, based strictly on my optimistic outlook. Of course, it's good to be optimistic, but not so good for Wall Street.

LL: Over-projecting profits can cost money.

The Merrill Lynch bankers met with us in February 1997, just when we were concerned that the demand for nutritional cheese and fat-free cheese was ebbing. We had used our advertising effectively on the fat-free product, knowing that the umbrella effect would increase interest in our other products as well. Still, the interest in the entire category was down, even in the entire market of cheese in general. (Note: In later years, cheese interest came back strong.)

We had hired an outside consultant at that time with a strong background in business, who was to become our CEO, with the idea of moving us toward a major nutritional deli line of foods. If we were selling

$110 million in cheese, we would sell $300 million in turkey, $200 million in roast beef, and $200 million in ham or salads. We had the plan laid out and ready to be implemented. Our consultant was committed to his role, but the entire plan was contingent on not selling the company.

At this point, we still had our cheese trading company doing about $30 million a year, and Alpine Lace, doing about $110 million annually.

1997 was slated to be a stable year for milk prices. We had just finished a tight year, so we knew the commodity cycle was in the right place.

Merrill Lynch gave us their presentation, telling us they could sell our company for $11–$15 a share. My goal had been $20 per share, but their estimation was still a lot of money. I owned 2.2 million shares. We gave them the authorization to start soliciting companies.

In March, just as they were putting everything together, Land O' Lakes approached Merrill Lynch with an offer to buy us at $8 a share.

Merrill Lynch told us, "It's a great deal."

We said, "What happened?"

"Well," they explained. "When we analyzed it, we decided this is what you can get, and you should take it."

"I don't know," I said. "It's way below where I wanted to be."

They went back to Land O' Lakes, which offered me a five-year non-compete clause at a million dollars a year, totaling $5 million, which translated to an additional $2.50 a share, bringing the sale up to $10.50 per share for me, but what about our key employees? They had very few stock options in the deal.

On a Thursday in June, we sat down with the board. When I expressed my concern for a shareholder lawsuit on my sweetheart $5 million non-compete, our SEC lawyer said, "Your company is too small, so you're not likely to be sued."

The deal was to be announced the following Monday. But the lawyer's words didn't sit well with either Marion or me. "I don't want to go out that way," I said to Marion.

On Saturday, when Marion and I talked again, we found we'd both come to the same decision. We called our contact at Land O' Lakes and said, "We're not going to do the deal."

Our contact was a good man. He was shocked but understood our position. At the same time, Marion and I realized we'd never done a proper discovery. What was the company worth? Did Merrill Lynch know? Did they have the facts? No, they had shortcut the process. We went back to them and said, "Listen, we want to proceed with an auction. Find out our value."

They agreed and went through the extensive process. In the subsequent auction, Land O' Lakes came back with the highest offer of $9.25 per share. At the same time, we put in two million shares of options for our employees as well as "stay" bonuses. Then, Land O' Lakes also offered me $2.5 million for non-competition.

Better.

We were now selling the company for what it was worth; no more pipe dreams of $20 a share. We were getting a fair return, and I was going out the right way, being fair to the shareholders and the people who worked for me.

We signed the deal in September 1997 and closed on a Friday in December. On Saturday, I walked into my office for the last time and cleaned out everything that was personal to me. I left with the sense of a job well done. I had accomplished everything professionally. I had taken care of my key employees, I had procured the best value for my shareholders, and my $2.5 million noncompete was also fair.

LL: The process of gaining information maximized our results and let us know we had done it correctly.

I left, looking forward to the next phase of my career: my "superstar" phase.

LL: Don't fall too much in love with yourself.

CHAPTER 20

Alpine Lace Lessons

One of the things I'd particularly liked doing at Alpine Lace was talking to investors and doing public relations. I thought of it as a discipline that spurred me to constantly do better. And if our stock was doing better, it was a measure of our performance, both a validation and a reward.

I only had one problem with investor relations: I found it slightly addictive. I spent quite a bit of my time talking to potential investors throughout the country. On a cross-country trip, I might visit five or six potential investors, or I would give a presentation on Alpine Lace at a large conference of up to seventy or more people.

When rumors first surfaced about the potential sale of our company, our stock went up, but when we showed losses a few years later, the stock dropped dramatically, from $16 to $2 per share. Naturally, I was concerned and hired an investor coach.

I asked her, "Who's going to buy our stock?"

She said. "Someone will buy your stock, but it will be a different type of buyer."

She was right. People still bought, and the stock came back to $7 a share. However, during that time, I was probably too focused on the share price. As a result, I was also too willing to listen to advice I should not have entertained.

I hired a devout Jew who put a mezuzah (a piece of parchment inscribed with specific Hebrew verses from the Torah) beside the door to my office. You're supposed to kiss the middle finger of your right hand and touch it to the mezuzah before you open the door, and that is supposed to bring you good luck.

This man also told me that he knew people in the Jewish religious community who would buy my stock on his recommendation, and it would do very well.

I should have heard the alarm bells go off: *Too good to be true!*

At that time, the stock was sitting at about $7. It didn't budge. However, he had options on company shares as part of his payment plan. When I fired him, I refused to give him his options because I felt he was a devout fraud who had bamboozled me, and so I appointed myself "the captain of morality," determined to punish him for his transgressions.

I hired a lawyer, and we went to arbitration. I said to my lawyer, "We should do some research and find other people he made the same promise to."

My lawyer counseled against it. "I don't recommend it. It's not going to be allowed."

Okay then. I simply did the research on my own and found some people who had had the same experience—the same promises of results that had never materialized.

At the arbitration session, I accused him of telling us he would "park the stock," meaning he would place the stock with his friends, and then, when the stock went up, his friends would sell.

"Are you accusing me of doing something illegal?" he said. "I would never do that!"

My lawyer, meanwhile, didn't say a word. There was nothing he could say without implicating our side in illegal activity. And I couldn't use the testimony I'd gathered from other people because I had never properly documented it.

We lost the arbitration ruling, and it cost me $250,000 in value, but it could have been worse. I could have lost up to $800,000.

Still, I was utterly livid. If I'd been a cartoon character, smoke would have been coming out of my ears. I was intensely consumed by this one incident that was completely irrelevant to our growth as a company.

LL: Don't get waylaid by a moral crusade you're not going to win. Even if you do win, it's not going to do anything for your business.

One other interesting incident occurred during that period. Kraft Foods threatened to sue us for false advertising. I suspect they were just being vindictive toward a much smaller company winning customers from their turf.

Our advertising said, "Our fat-free American Singles are made with real cheddar cheese." Kraft insisted this was false because fat-free cheese had not yet been defined.

Someone on our board called a person he knew in the cheese division at Kraft. "Hey! What's going on? What can we do?"

"We don't like the ad."

"Can we change it?"

The answer was yes, and we made a tweak that made Kraft happy and kept us out of trouble. The new wording turned out to be just as effective.

"Our American Singles are made with real Cheddar flavor."

LL: Sometimes you have to let people win. Decide what's important and focus on that.

We also had another small "issue" with Kraft. We had a low-sodium product so did Kraft. They said they were beating us in taste tests. Well, everybody freaked out. I said, "Relax, on a scale of 1-10, we're an 8.5; Kraft is a 9. But 8.5 is good." And it was. Our product continued to do well.

CHAPTER 21

The Next Phase

Marion was always a terrific asset to our business and, of course, to me. Near the end of our Alpine Lace venture, we started recognizing that relationship and developed a campaign on copreneurship, a term that refers to a married couple jointly owning, managing, and operating a business, and sharing responsibilities and decisions while intertwining their work and family lives. It's a business model that can foster a supportive environment with shared goals. For Marion and me, it was a tremendous success. In our partnership at that time, Marion was often the star.

At a milestone annual meeting held at the new LA Fitness Club in New York City's West Side, Marion gave a summary speech of our accomplishments and was tremendously well-received.

LL: Let a capable partner be noticed and recognized.

After the sale of Alpine Lace, I noticed that Land O' Lakes was not following the good rules under which we had operated the company. For about two weeks, I was upset; upset enough that I was complaining about it while Marion and I were having dinner with another couple.

But I finally said, "You know, it's over. They're going to do what they're going to do."

Land O' Lakes didn't want to hear from me, and they certainly didn't want me in the building. This was their baby now, and they thought they knew everything. I did contact the person I'd dealt with at

Land O' Lakes, explaining the four major things they were messing up on. They'd spent millions of dollars to buy us, and then threw out our distribution network, quality procedures, and sources of supply, and fired our entire sales network within the first month. Land O' Lakes wrote off most of the value of the purchase a few years later.

LL: Pay attention to the virtues of the company you are buying and wait until making changes that are carefully thought out.

I had my say and moved on.

My next phase was all about sitting on boards and investing, mainly in communications companies. I hired a consultant to introduce me to private equity hedge funds that bought companies with the idea that I would be running the acquisitions.

I also believed I would be a "hot property," sought after by many companies to sit on their boards, particularly food companies, my area of expertise. I had a great background in everything from finance and marketing to sales, SEC compliance, short raids, and raising capital. I was a "catch."

The consultant contacted a number of private equity firms, but only a few showed interest, particularly one in San Francisco, whose project would have me searching out acquisitions and running them—with one catch: I would have to invest about $2 million into the purchases and in return, I would own about 15 percent of the company, while the equity firm would own the rest.

I said no for several reasons. First, I had been living on a modest income before the sale of Alpine Lace. Now that I had some cash, I didn't want to risk it. Second, I knew I would have to fly all around the country, and that was something I didn't want to do. I also didn't want to answer to an equity firm. Essentially, they would be my boss, and I would have no control.

I also didn't receive any major board offers. I didn't understand it and I wasn't happy about it, until one of the board members at Alpine Lace, who had worked at General Foods and went on to become the CEO of Saks department stores, explained to me, "You're very, very entrepreneurial, and that scares people."

In other words, I wasn't a "corporate guy."

I wasn't ready to be done with business. I wanted to step into my next phase: my grand phase! One of my options was to become the "horse" for a private equity firm; another was to join up with a fellow entrepreneur to buy distressed companies. I considered incubating small companies, buying a diner in my hometown, and getting involved in a business group of high-net-worth peers. I jumped into all of them.

I started buying into small companies with a low-risk investment of about $100,000 in each, creating an incubator for mostly software and internet marketing businesses. In most of these, I served as advisor, and was on the board of a few.

I invested in a total of seven businesses, one of which was a grand slam, returning more than $1 million after selling out to AOL within a year. When I first met with the CEO, he just talked and talked, wound up as tight as an inner spring. He was smart, he had all the knowledge, but he seemed unable to take a breath.

I finally said, "Thanks. I'm not investing."

His jaw dropped. "Why not?"

"Because you're not listening. You're so busy telling your story, you're not open to hearing others or to learning anything new.

"You know," he said. "You're right. I'm sorry."

His willingness to be honest at that point was enough to persuade me to invest.

His company was in the business of purchasing ad space on all the major platforms, like Google, AOL, and others. They then sold that space to other companies. Simply put, it was a form of arbitrage, and they made an excellent margin.

LL: When you invest in start-up companies, the risk is much higher, but the reward is also much higher.

I soon discovered that most of the entrepreneurs who ran these companies I invested in were often afraid to make changes. In some cases, they were completely stuck. Maybe they thought that whatever they'd been doing to get them where they were had worked, and they'd better not change that formula. Some of their ideas were good. One company had an internet site that matched up roommates and also comparison shopped bank credit cards. They could have gone far. Unfortunately, the person running the company was insecure. His team was good, but he was holding them back.

The same guy also put together a word-processing program for newspapers, which was also a good idea, but he was stuck.

LL: Often, people will have excellent ideas, but when it comes time to implement change, they are too afraid to mess with what they already have, even when change is necessary for growth.

Of the seven businesses I invested in, only one was a grand slam; with one, we got our money back; and I became the chairman of one called Conduit-IT, after bringing in friends as investors. Conduit built virtual catalogues for industrial companies like Sherwin-Williams, listing every type of industrial paint and accessory on the market, making it easy for them to manage their SKUs, or stockkeeping units. Conduit-IT also made it easy to change the catalogue and input new data. Marion got quite involved in that company, as did one of my friends who sat on the board.

The company president was a charming young man, but eventually, he couldn't take the pressure and left. I stepped in as interim CEO. I knew nothing about writing software, but still had to fill his shoes and make presentations to major customers. Happily, I did fine, partly because I left discussion of the technical details to other members of the team.

We eventually brought in a new CEO and sold the company at a small loss. I may have ended up losing a small amount of money, but I learned a good deal by directing all the aspects of the operation.

LL: Possibly, the most important thing I learned is that when you're a consultant or an advisor, many times your advice is not followed, especially if you're advising young people. In fact, many people will ask for advice, but they won't follow it. I didn't learn how to get buy-in until much later.

One of my more interesting ventures was sitting on the board of a company originally called Books on Tape, and then Books on CDs, before becoming Mediabay. When the CFO brought me in, the company was doing about $40 million in business, selling programs similar to a book-of-the-month club. In this case, it was a tape-of-the-month club (shortly becoming books on CDs). For $1, you could get seven books on tape. After that, you would pay $12 a month for a year. Members could opt out and send back the books after three months.

The business was earning about $4 million annually. I can only describe the chairman as very hands-on. He owned it and involved his family, including two sons. Early on in my involvement, he decided to step back and simply be an investor while I stepped into his place.

However, the now-former chair and owner had 40% of the company shares, and his strong personality cut through everything. I thought I was a man with a strong presence; he was much more dominant.

In my new role, it became apparent that the core business of the company was topping. Acquiring new customers wasn't that hard, but retaining them was tough. The company believed in the philosophy of Lifetime Value of a Customer, which includes the cost of acquiring them, and that included seven virtually free books plus marketing costs. Over time, the purchases repaid the original cost, and in the end, if the customer stayed, they were profitable.

They were experts at utilizing the internet for acquiring new customers by buying ad space in all the right places, but the market was changing, and customers started leaving early, or not paying, or returning the product.

I told them, "You have great marketing skills. You're a public company on NASDAQ. Let's buy other small profitable direct marketing companies selling items like gold coins or constitutional artifacts." My point was that we could buy these companies at low acquisition costs and expand the business very profitably.

With the core business of books on disc waning, I saw this as a golden opportunity. We could buy the companies and, over time, get our money back because we could greatly expand the business with our marketing skills. Unfortunately, the company owner said no. He was looking at other wild ideas, but none of them were germane to our business and none would take advantage of our unique marketing skills.

In time, and as predicted, the business began to falter. We were looking at refinancing when we showed a profit of $1 million for the quarter, but some numbers had changed to now show a loss of $1 million a month later. We had a 20% change in income within 30 days, and that was unacceptable. I terminated our key operating person over that. He was smart, but he was breaking the rules.

LL: The numbers should never lie and should be on time. If you fudge, it makes it worse, and your first loss is your best loss. Believe the numbers.

We searched for and hired a new CEO, who didn't work out after three months. Meanwhile, we were trying to raise $5 million, and I had torn a tendon playing tennis and was in a cast. I went to the investment banker, told them our CEO was no longer with us, and I was the interim CEO. They didn't bat an eye and proceeded to raise the capital.

That was good, but we still had the issue of our core business faltering. I realized then that no matter what title I had, I would not be able to override the owner. I was working on a deal to sell the company to Audible, bought by Amazon in 2008. It was an attractive deal, but the owner and major shareholder wanted more—too much—and the deal fell through.

I left. They thought I'd deserted them, but the fact was, I was not free to implement any of my ideas. Eventually, the company shut down.

LL: When the facts are staring you in the face, it's time to make a hard decision and move on. I liked Mediabay, but they were not realistic about their operations and future.

CHAPTER 22

Blue Moon

The Blue Moon diner was an adventure we bought in 1999. I was busy with a lot of things, so my idea was to come into the local diner, say hello to everyone, sit down, drink coffee, talk to the customers, and have a terrific time. That would be the total scope of my involvement.

What is it they say about the best-laid plans?

The Blue Moon diner was not what I had imagined it to be. Chef after chef was either incompetent, drunk, or just quit. Then the hot water heater didn't work, and then the manager wasn't trustworthy and we fired him on a Friday with the understanding our new manager would start on Monday. He never showed up. "Marion," I said. "I'm closing the diner."

She thought that was a bad idea. "No, you're not. You bought it. You own it. You're going to run it until we straighten it out."

So, we stuck with it and turned it into a diner/café, upgrading every item on the menu.

Suddenly, the Blue Moon became so popular, we'd have people lined up down the street. People came for excellent food with innovative, progressive dishes. Sometimes people might have to wait for their order, but they didn't mind because they knew they would be served only the best quality food.

My son-in-law, Matt Brown, who had worked for General Foods, said he wanted to manage the diner. Great! He became a partner. Matt was very responsible, personable, articulate, and smart. Family businesses often have a reputation for a lot of in-fighting and unrest. We never had that issue. Matt was more conservative than me and tempered some of my more exuberant ideas. He was the rational, logical partner, but we were always united in how we wanted to run the diner, and later, our appetizer business, and our Mama's Creations NASDAQ-listed company. Only once or twice did we have a disagreement that lasted for perhaps a day or two before blowing over.

He was the person who made solid, complete, and articulate presentations to the board and others. He was a great asset to our joint business relationship.

We sold the diner/café in 2001. During that time, we made it the place to be. I did a lot of local marketing, and we gave people a reason to keep coming back.

We had outdoor seating for about seven tables. We decorated with tons of potted flowers and brought in a band one night a week. We had square dancing, charity events, and free Thanksgiving breakfasts. We had contests for kids, pancake-eating contests, and major displays that changed with the seasons, like hay bales and scarecrows in the fall.

We hung 15–18 decorative banners from the ceiling that changed with the season or the occasion; we had flags for Halloween, Thanksgiving, Christmas, winter, St. Patrick's Day, Easter, spring, July Fourth, and summer; about eight or nine changes of banners.

People genuinely appreciated us. But even after we were running smoothly, I never did get to walk in, say hello, and relax. I'd go in Saturday mornings and drive to the wholesaler's if we were short of food. In the afternoon, I'd watch the place, and on Saturday evenings,

I'd come in at about 11 p.m., close it down, count the money, and reconcile the books.

I watched the weekly numbers. In fact, if you run a small business, it can be very satisfying to run those numbers through your fingers and know exactly where you are. We had a significantly positive cash flow.

When we changed the name of the Blue Moon from diner to diner/café, that's how we advertised it. I bought a big billboard on the highway that showcased Blue Moon as voted the number one diner/café in New Jersey.

One person said to me, "How is that possible?"

"Well," I answered. "We're the only one in the state."

When the store next door in our small strip mall left, and we had the opportunity to expand, we didn't take it. It was a lot of work and we were done.

In the spring of 2001, my son-in-law, Matt, and I bought Hors d'oeuvres Unlimited. At the time, I was still involved in Mediabay and a number of other incubating companies, and also with investments with my peer business group in New York City. I had a lot of energy in those days.

I think I may have been caught up in a frenzy of activity and enterprises in a bid to prove myself again and show the world I wasn't done. When we sold Alpine Lace, I'd done well, but it was definitely time to leave. Still, I didn't feel totally accomplished. I had another mountain to climb.

During this hectic period in my life, I was climbing that other mountain.

LL: Today, I believe that after you hit a major milestone, it might be better to just let things settle down before deciding your next step.

Instead of doing that, I pivoted because I was churning internally, wanting to dive immediately into my next phase, and the small entrepreneurs accepted me. I was on the board or advisory board (consultant) in several smaller companies, including software for the Armed Forces, programmed trading, gourmet cheeses, and start-ups/turnarounds. I was busy. And at least in part, they were listening to my advice because I had skin in the game. I'd invested money.

I wanted to be important. Even though Alpine Lace was very successful, deep inside, I felt we hadn't achieved what I'd hoped for. We'd maximized what we had, but if I'm going to be honest, I was disappointed with the end result.

Perhaps this next phase I found myself in was about personal redemption.

CHAPTER 23

Hors d'oeuvres Unlimited and Mama Mancini's

I learned a lot of lessons from Alpine Lace.

LL: If you're going to choose a career path or a business path, you should go into a positive environment that is growing and where the competition is honest. You want to make sure your choice is one where you can make margins and profits, and, if you make mistakes (which you will), the positive aspects of the business will carry you.

Many people will make bad choices. For example, opening a hair salon two doors down from another one, or a bakery on the same block as another. Sometimes, people will go into an industry with no great prospects of growth and poor pay. You have to slow down, think about your options, and not jump blindly at an opportunity even if it's expedient in the short run.

I was fortunate when I entered the restaurant business. I didn't have the right partner, but the roll-up concept was correct. In the case of Alpine Lace, we were in a dynamic, growing nutritional foods industry. I had weak competition, which allowed us to grow dramatically, and in the case of my investments and entrepreneurial businesses, I was always looking for a unique niche. The software and internet advisory roles were profitable and presented a great teaching and learning experience, but I dropped out when the prospects proved too difficult.

In 2001, partnering with my son-in-law, Matt, I thought I'd found another one of those interesting niche businesses that would do well. And at $500,000, the price was right. Hors d'oeuvres Unlimited was a fairly small plant in North Bergen, New Jersey, doing $2 million in business annually, supplying about 200 hotels, restaurants, institutions, and caterers.

The plant was old and inadequate. When the entrance suffered during a major flood, we knew we had to move. So we built a much larger plant in East Rutherford, about eight miles away, but in doing so, we made a major mistake.

Our employees were immigrants, mainly from Central America, who lived in the area and either walked to work or took the bus. We had no direct bus route to the new plant. We either had to pick up our employees in a van or hire new local people at a 20% increase in wages.

We had a few other issues as well, mainly that the old facility was inadequate for our growth prospects. And then, we took up a big million-dollar school lunch program for turkey hot dogs, which we could run in a separate evening shift for one easy product. The hot dogs were wrapped like a big frank-in-a-blanket, but the well-known national turkey frank supplier had given us a batch with black plastic mixed into the meat. We had to recall all the franks, and the turkey company refused to take any responsibility.

So here we were in a new plant without substantial new business and with higher labor costs and much higher rent, overheads, utility bills, insurance, and equipment costs. Where the business had been marginally profitable in the old plant, it started losing a substantial amount of money. The new plant's capacity was five times the old one; we needed new customers. To do that, we unwisely lowered our margins and took on business that was not profitable—short notice orders, customers who made a lot of deductions, and those who didn't pay on time.

LL: When the going gets rough, slow down and don't panic. We should have lowered our costs until we developed a profitable business.

In 2006, Dan Mancini, a gentleman from South Orange, came into our plant to tell us, "I have the world's greatest meatball. It's my grandma, Mama Mancini's recipe."

We were curious enough to bring it to our executive chef, who tested it and confirmed that it was indeed a really delicious meatball. Unbelievably delicious, in fact. We added it to our line. At about the same time, we added upscale appetizers from well-known chefs on the East Coast.

Unfortunately, the special items didn't really take off. People buying from us were more interested in mid-level appetizers. Typically, a caterer would employ two or three chefs, who worked for them during the slow months when they made most of the appetizers themselves. During the busiest months of April, May, June, and then October, November, and December, they leaned heavily on our appetizers rather than hiring more chefs.

It was a bit of a whiplash business, but by 2008, we'd grown it from $2 million to about $8 million, and we had some pretty good customers. Yes, we were still losing money, but we had goals and they looked highly obtainable. We had started a major online appetizer business, called Appetizers to Go, bringing in 300,000 monthly visitors in November and December. We also developed a custom label business with high-end gourmet names like Neiman-Marcus and Williams-Sonoma.

Still, the fact that our business was skewed toward the holidays proved problematic. For two months, we'd be running flat out, and then, in January, we'd hit a slump.

Then, the major recession hit in September 2008, and people did not want to entertain. The general attitude in the country was, "How can you have a party when things are so bad?"

We lost about a third of our business. The crisis was bad enough that we considered closing shop, especially when an outside business consultant recommended that we shut the doors. But between the buildup of the new plant, the closing down of the old plant, the losses we'd sustained, and working capital, our investment at this point was about $4–$5 million. I thought about the consultant's advice, weighed it all in, and said, "No."

I called in another consultant, my friend and mentor, Richard Lavin. I'd known him for years through several business groups he ran, and I trusted him as a good business coach.

He said, "You know, the best thing you have is those meatballs. You should be marketing them under your brand, instead of all the private label stuff you're doing, and really promote them."

That's how Mama Mancini's began. We started slowly and with the basics. Dan Mancini was a terrific salesman who decided to work with us but not take an interest in the company, opting for royalties instead. Through trial and error, we grew the business.

In retrospect, I find it interesting that I did not follow the tried-and-true rules I'd lived by with Alpine Lace. For instance, we didn't invest a lot of money in market research. Basically, everything I did was alien to what I had learned years ago.

One thing we had going for us was a great product. Our sales grew to about $2 million, and I raised about $600,000 to further develop the line. As we grew, we converted part of our hors d'oeuvres plant into a partial meatball plant. The plant started breaking even. Then we found an investment banker. Spartan Capital Securities, which loved what we were doing and agreed to raise capital for us at a valuation of $20 million. We were one of the earliest of Spartan's clients and a good one, too. In 2012, we raised $5 million and continued to do well.

Mama Mancini's became a good, lucrative business, but somewhere along the way, I believe I should have paused for a moment to review what I had learned in the past. Maybe it was because I was protecting my assets that I forgot my basic principles.

Our most profitable trade in the appetizers business was selling to caterers, restaurants, and institutions that staged parties. I should have offered them free goods for a month to build the business. Years ago, I had done that successfully in the cheese business. Or I should have offered special incentives like trips and prizes, or contests. I didn't do that either.

While all this was going on with Mama Mancini's, I still had my other internet incubator ventures and was on the board of Mediabay, so perhaps I wasn't making Mama Mancini's enough of a priority. Still, I was not following my own rules. I was too focused on preserving the money I had.

Honestly, by 2008, my portfolio had grown substantially. I'd invested in various companies for a total of $5 million, but even so, my portfolio was 33% higher than it had been in 2000.

But there we were in 2008 in a recession, and I lost about 33% of my portfolio— perhaps more—and I got depressed. Not as badly as I was in 1977, though, and I got over it all right.

So the value of Mama Mancini's had grown substantially by 2012. Along the way, we had a difficult stretch, but by 2012, I was back on the ball, functioning the way I expected myself to.

LL: Sometimes you forget the life lessons you learn. It may be a good idea every now and then to take stock. I didn't. It's only now, as I'm writing this and looking back, that I see what I did, and how I forgot what I should have known. I think it's better to take stock earlier rather than later.

CHAPTER 24

Mama Mancini's – The Highs and Lows

As Mama Mancini's grew, we allocated a considerable amount of money to sales and brand development. We were building a brand, and if we were losing money, that was part of our strategy.

We expanded our sales force and paid for major new placement fees and very high promotional programs. As a result, we started doing business with the big guns: Costco, Sam's Club, Walmart, and other major chains right across the country.

We also started doing substantial business with QVC, the largest direct-to-consumer television network and a flagship shopping channel specializing in televised home shopping. At the same time, we expanded our lines.

Our board was a bit unusual in that it consisted mainly of investors who knew each other, rather than experts in various fields like accounting or law. At one point later in our existence, the board asked that Marion resign as a member because they felt there were too many family members.

LL: Our family owned controlling equity in the business, and I should have refused and lived with the consequences. We lost a valuable asset.

We went public in 2012, raising $3 million more in capital in 2015. In 2016, we were in the process of raising another $15 million on a company valuation of $70 million, using BTIG Capital, a global financial services firm specializing in investment banking, institutional trading, and research. Our aim was to build a major consumer packaged goods brand.

However, even though the product was a 10 out of 10, our process was labor-intensive and time-consuming, and in order to make the product viable for production in large quantities, we had to change the recipe and the production process. With the change, we still had a very good product, but it was now an 8 out of 10.

Then we brought in some outside investors for Meatball Obsession, the new food service retail arm of Mama Mancini's, which operated out of a kiosk. Mama Mancini's wound up owning 28% of the new enterprise.

Interestingly, I probably had more restaurant and retail knowledge than anyone on the board or in the company, but was not asked to be involved in the decision-making on the new food service venture.

I saw serious issues with the operating decisions being made for Meatball Obsession. The quality of the bread was just one of them. What's more, bread deliveries only arrived every second or third day, so the bread was often not fresh. The first kiosk was in New York, and in New York, of all places, the establishment had no seating available.

Perhaps the biggest issue was not listening to the customer. We made a mellow meatball, not a spicy one, and young New Yorkers, who were the most likely to frequent a fast-food kiosk, wanted spicy meatballs.

I wanted to develop Grandpa's Spicy Balls. That didn't happen. And then, another small adjustment would have made a big difference. Because the meatballs were pretty large, it looked like you weren't getting a lot of bang for your buck. I wanted to make them medium-sized: give people twice as many and increase the perceived value.

It also took too long to prepare them, and we served them in cups. No spaghetti and meatballs in a cup or even a salad to go with them.

We certainly got a lot of publicity and interest in what we were doing, with initial lines down the block, but the customers were rating us 3 out of 5. The biggest complaints were around the lack of a spicy meatball option, the bread, and the perceived value.

LL: Some people, when given power, change their modus operandi. You have to be careful not to let that happen to you. If you're involved, you have to be assertive.

We were the developers of the idea and the suppliers of the meatballs. We should have asserted our position. Sadly, we didn't do that.

The idea was to open a nationwide chain of Meatball Obsession kiosks. They opened a second in a mall, but it failed. We opened several more at highway rest stops, which were also unsuccessful. The product was okay, but only just okay, and still, they weren't listening to the customers.

On paper, however, we were looking good. Mama Mancini's was gearing up to open thousands of meatball shops, and in terms of valuation, that projection was adding a lot of value.

John Lowry of Spartan Capital, who had become a friend, was all for raising new capital through BTIG, a larger investment banker, but everybody got greedy, and the deal placement slowed down. Then, just at that crucial point, I developed psoriatic arthritis, which was misdiagnosed. All I knew at the time was that I had severe inflammation in all my joints and was in such terrible pain, I could barely move. The doctors believed I had problems with my arteries and prescribed 80 mg of prednisone, an extreme dose.

The dosage alleviated the swelling, but the side effects were horrendous. I became irascible and short-tempered. I also had a hard time sleeping, so I'd be up in the middle of the night, writing memos at 3 a.m.

I developed a combative relationship with BTIG's attorneys and with my board. Eventually, I was properly diagnosed, and my prednisone prescription was lowered to 20 mg. But that wasn't until March 2017. In November 2016, I wasn't an easy person to get along with.

The deal for our additional financing was supposed to go through in mid-November, but the bank pulled it two days before it was to be completed. We had $500,000 in the bank, and were deliberately losing $350,000 per month on heavy sales and promotion, and we owed about $750,000 to lawyers and accountants who had been working on the deal. Our accounts payable were $1.2 million.

LL: No one likes failure, and when the proverbial s**t hits the fan, blame gets spread around everywhere. When things are good, everyone's happy, but when things go wrong, everyone is unhappy and looking for someone to pin it on.

Spartan had been counting on a new cash infusion for us. They were not happy. I got a phone call that devolved into a one-hour harangue. I was seriously ill and just barely functioning. I was driving home, listening to a blast of words. When I arrived, I put the phone away, got out of my car, and walked into my apartment. I picked up the phone ten minutes later, and the guy was still ranting.

But here's the thing: no matter how bad things get, you keep doing what you have to do. In late December, I found $2 million in other financing. It almost fell apart when it got testy between both sets of lawyers, but I fully interceded and got the funds.

At some point during all this, we picked up a new board member who was in the financing industry. That was good news. Real potential! But when he saw the numbers and the infighting, he got out. His first meeting as a board member was the day of our annual Christmas party. After the meeting, he said, "This is not for me." He didn't show up at the party and we were in shock. He did, however, buy some of our stock later.

But I knew how to make this work. I conserved capital, figuring out who to pay and when. I paid off the debt slowly, or put it on hold, or turned some of it into equity, stabilized the company, and changed the course of the business. Instead of trying to build a retail brand, I turned our focus to the deli.

At this point, I needed to raise more money, but I was also furious about how I'd been treated by Spartan. I fired them and hired a new firm, William Smith & Company, in Denver, Colorado. Then I traveled around the country trying to raise capital, but came up empty-handed. I could barely function, but slogged through anyway, traveling across the country to make presentations to potential investors.

William Smith & Company's lawyer then declared we were bankrupt and refused to approve a financing application. We also had a disagreement with the principal's daughter. I suspect her father's displeasure about that had something to do with the company's decision. Not surprisingly, we parted ways.

At that point, Spartan showed interest again, and we scheduled a major call-in board meeting. Spartan's John Lowry and I were talking on the phone earlier in the day. The conversation had been positive as to a plan of action, but that changed when the meeting began. That's when all the anger that had been building inside him for months erupted. He spent a good half-hour telling me and everyone else that I was an awful executive.

I was blindsided. Though completely stunned, I sat and took it.. Internally, I was close to erupting as well. Then one of my board members said, "We're going to have to check this out, all these allegations."

I exploded. My wife and son-in-law, who were also on the board at the meeting, started yelling right alongside me. In under sixty seconds, it became a free-for-all, like something out of a *Mad Men* scene.

I said, "I'm out of here," and hung up. My board was very concerned, and that was probably because they weren't professional board people. They were investors.

If there were high and low points in Mama Mancini's history, I'd call that *the* low point. But I pulled myself together because I still had to raise capital, and I did everything I needed to in order to keep the business going: cut expenses, paid in stock rather than cash where I could, and held onto payables. While I was doing my damndest, our corporate lawyer was telling my board that he wasn't sure about my competency.

By this point, I was down to 20 mg of prednisone, and I could see that he was basing his judgments on our interactions when I was taking 80 mg. True, I hadn't been a fully rational person then. However, my son-in-law Matt and I owned 40% of the stock. What did the board think it was going to do? And why was my lawyer raising these concerns now? Why not come to me and say, "Carl, let's go over some things?"

But he didn't, so I made a smart move: I hired another lawyer, brought him into a meeting with my corporate lawyer, and addressed his concerns. My new lawyer refuted every accusation, and I walked out of the meeting victorious. And then I hired a new corporate lawyer.

LL: You have to pick yourself up. You're going to get hurt at times. Rethink and do what you have to do if you're going to be a successful entrepreneur.

I kept doing what I had to do, and by April 2017, we broke even on cash flow. We still needed money. John Lowry felt I'd betrayed him, and

I felt he'd let me down. He wrote a letter of apology to my wife and son-in-law.

Me? I forgave him. John and I were close enough that I could let it go, and we're still friends.

In 2017, because we still needed money, I put up $500,000. My son-in-law put up $50,000. The board put up $200,000, some friends put up $300,000, and one stockbroker at Spartan found investors and raised enough to bring us up to $2.2 million.

Now we had enough capital and changed the company focus from branded retail and partial deli case, to almost exclusively deli case. The margins in the deli case were much higher, while promotions and losses were much less. The volume per location was also higher. Our product was very good, and soon we developed ancillary products. That was the good news.

Of course, there was also bad news. The deli case sold only one brand of meatballs. In order to get in there, you had to supplant the one already featured. Sometimes, the store had its own recipe, or they had tried a brand in the past and it had failed, and they were reluctant to go down that road again.

The window of opportunity was a narrow one. Still, we moved into the deli cases one retail chain at a time, developing a lot of new business slowly and steadily. We started making money. We also found that just as with Alpine Lace, our relationships with the buyers were important. Often, the buyers were clerks who had moved up the ladder. To them, the numbers were important, as well as the relationships.

We called on our sales agencies, which had relationships with the buyers, to get our product in. When we did get it in, it sold. Over time, we added sausages, turkey meatballs, and pasta dishes, each one a successful expansion of our line.

We also started advertising on Sirius radio, leaning again on lessons we'd learned at Alpine Lace. We bought time at attractive rates. True—radio is not a great medium when you're selling to consumers, but it's very effective when you are advertising to the trade.

If we were in a room with five people on the buying team, two would have heard our ads on Sirius. We would bundle our ad into a four or six-week period around holidays when rates were also much lower, and we were given thousands of free spots. For about $125,000 a year, we were very effective in selling to the trade.

We also developed a special presentation program. Since our meatballs were in a red sauce, we had a red tablecloth, a beautiful pull-up sign, red plates and napkins, fine serving utensils, beautiful white dishes, and a gorgeous brochure. The impression we made was "Wow! These people are first class!"

And then, our secret weapon was a sales agent who had a good relationship with the buyers.

LL: A steady, consistent strategy and diligence can pay off big. Dig in and don't get discouraged.

Over time, we developed more and more of those important relationships, and we got more business. By 2018-2019, we were making a decent amount of money. Then COVID hit in 2020, and it turned out to be a tremendous boon for us. People were no longer going out to eat at restaurants. Instead, they were buying prepared foods in supermarkets. Our business was very strong. Along with our meatballs, we were selling all our other products as well, like chicken parmesan and penne pasta.

Sam's Club became a huge customer. We were one of a handful of suppliers who could fill their need for product. People were stocking up on huge quantities in order to limit their shopping trips. Our meatloaf and chicken parmesan were our two major items, flying off the shelves.

But then commodity prices for chicken and beef skyrocketed. We were being squeezed, but managed to get through it by raising our prices enough to remain profitable. However, we were getting feedback that our chicken parmesan product was mediocre. The buyer, who was not an easy person to please, warned us that the product was an issue. Still, the volume of sales had doubled, so we kept shipping without making changes.

By October 2020, we lost Sam's chicken parmesan business. We were still doing okay, but we should have paid closer attention.

LL: When you know something isn't right, do something about it. We didn't, and we paid the price. We were too busy basking in the glory of high sales volumes.

CHAPTER 25

Mama Mancini's Crises and Evolution

Business wasn't all gloomy. We continued developing other customers. QVC was particularly strong. Still, when commodity prices went up, we were feeling the pinch.

And then I learned a big life lesson. I became fascinated by meme stocks, which are essentially stocks like AMC Theaters or GameStop that have gone viral in the same way a funny photo or video can get passed around the internet. People were at home, had some extra Covid money, and were playing the market.

In anticipation of getting listed on NASDAQ, I spent about $5,000 a month for three months, advertising on Facebook, Reddit, and other social media, inviting people to check out Mama Mancini's. "Look at our growth!"

In July 2021, we got uplisted to NASDAQ. On the day we uplisted, our stock, which had been averaging about 40,000 shares in trading volume, traded 23 million shares! The share price went from $2.45 to $11. The day was totally insane. The stock stopped trading twice; my phone didn't stop ringing all morning. The word was, "Mama Mancini's is going to the moon!"

At 3 p.m., all the people who had bought and pumped the stock up dumped it, and the stock went right back down to $2.45.

LL: I learned my lesson: Be careful. If you're going to get involved in a fad, you'd better know what you're doing.

I didn't know what I was doing and I didn't promote the stock. I just made people aware of it. The marketing concept worked, but I had to do more to hold the price up, like announcing potential deals. When you do something like this, you have to go farther and deeper. I just assumed that when we went public, we would garner more interest. I didn't expect anything like what we did get.

The telephone didn't ring at all after 3 p.m. Not one call. But in the big picture of Mama Mancini's, I had the grit and the determination. At one point, after the financing had collapsed a few years earlier, my family was willing to stop the company at 40 cents a share, which would have brought a total of $4 or $5 million.

I said, "No."

So, in mid-2021, I started searching for acquisitions to address our issues in the Italian food products business.

At that point, I hired an outside consultant. It can be helpful to hire a consultant for a specific, defined task. Working in the company on so many different fronts, it's easy to get diverted. The outside consultant is wearing blinders and is focused only on their specific task.

So, you hire a consultant who is knowledgeable and competent at the task. Then you define the project and guide them. Over the years, I have hired consultants to find new sources of products. One of the most successful was finding an excellent source of tomatoes in Ohio. No one knew you could get great tomatoes in Ohio. We also found a great pasta resource.

LL: A good consultant can be a great return on investment.

In this case, I used a consultant to help me with an acquisition. The consultant I principally used was Noel Ebrahim, and we're still good friends.

I had confidence in my ability to pick a good acquisition because I'd been an acquisitions manager in my early career. I applied search techniques I was familiar with, spreading my net wide and announcing publicly that we were doing a search. With any luck, we would be contacted. We obtained lists of companies we might want to buy and contacted business brokers, accounting firms, and lawyers.

We found about 15 serious possibilities, which I narrowed down to a company on Long Island, T&L Salads, that sold salads and grilled chicken, doing about $40 million in annual sales. We were doing about $48 million at the time. T&L had a rudimentary accounting system, but the principals were street smart, and I liked them.

My board, however, was completely against it. I paid no attention and pushed it through hard, and we bought it at a great price. I remembered the Life Lesson of S&H— that you need a sponsor to make it happen. We had the cash from prior profits, and with Noel Ebrahim's help, we did the pro forma financials and brought in an outside firm to do an analysis of the business. They concluded that the numbers didn't make sense. Okay, but I was convinced that I could develop higher sales and bigger profits.

But the most recent board member, the manager of a small hedge fund who had joined our board in 2020, was strongly opposed to the deal. He was an astute but challenging board member, more so when the company stopped showing a profit. He owned about 5% of the company stock and stepped in aggressively, trying to tell me how to proceed. I paid no attention to him. He hated the deal. I fired the lawyers he recommended because they wanted a perfect deal. That wasn't going to happen. I knew I would have to bend to make this work. The purchase price was good $3 million—and we had the cash.

What we didn't know at the time was that our accounting system was in shambles, and we had to review T&L's numbers, which were on a rudimentary QuickBooks cash flow system. We also had to look at the family expenses accounting and recast the numbers under our management. In addition, according to the SEC, we had to review T&L's books for the past three years. Given that they dealt generally on a cash basis, we had to reconstruct the entire business to have it make sense. Our accounting firm took a look and said, "We can't figure it out. We can't do it."

But without the review, we couldn't buy the company. I approached a small forensic accounting firm I'd dealt with previously that was able to figure out the numbers, and we made the deal. The company was earning about $500,000 annually. All in all, I figured it was a good transaction.

In 2021, Sam's Club told us they were delisting our meatloaf. It made no sense to us. It was a high-volume item—about $6 million in value—and a major blow.

As a company, we were doing about $50 million in annual sales with good products, so we'd be okay, but still, the Sam's announcement was a gut punch. The buyer at Sam's had always been challenging. She didn't like price increases, and our margins had already been lower. So now what? We were stagnating because, on top of everything else, we were being whiplashed by prices in the ground meat market. A desperate drought was putting ground meat in a tight supply situation, and cattle prices were predicted to go up.

At the same time, we were putting in a new accounting system, and it had issues and was not working as it should. In the spring of 2022, our accounting department had a $700,000 discrepancy that they could not reconcile. Between the loss of the Sam's business and bad accounting, our profits fell to zero.

And then in November 2021, doctors discovered I had a growth on my spine, which had to be removed. It was a low time for us. What was next?

In 2022, right after we made the acquisition, chicken prices hit the ceiling, and what were supposed to be profits became a barely break-even situation.

T&L also had an olive business, and olive prices went up. And then we had to deal with the same buyer at Sam's Club that we had with our meatloaf. As expected, the buyer resisted our price increases. T&L was ready to give up.

I said, "No. Prices will turn around."

The buyer did allow for small increases, but not enough. Her stand was to keep prices down for her customers. I could empathize, but the strategy wasn't practical. We had to make money. A large number of her suppliers were medium-sized, like us, so she could be firm about what she would or would not accept. A large supplier like Tyson could just walk away. We were stuck.

In April 2022, the accounting issues continued to plague us to the point where we couldn't issue our financial statements on time. I always believed in timely, honest, accurate numbers, and I was deeply upset. Unfortunately, it was out of my hands. When the company was smaller, I'd kept a close eye on the financials, daily and weekly. As we grew larger, I handed that responsibility to the accounting department. The fact that we were late meant a warning from NASDAQ. Not good! At the same time, our numbers weren't great. Still, I managed to convince NASDAQ to give us a 10-day extension, and we were in compliance two days later. I believe we averted a major disaster.

By June 2022, between the accounting issues and the chicken prices going crazy, and the meatball business being marginal, we were a break-even business. The investor board member who loved me when the stock was up, but not so much now, quit the board. He sold off his stock that summer and fall, depressing our price temporarily.

LL: Being a good investor in business is very different from being an operator.

LL: Sometimes you have to grind it out and make a whole lot of small decisions, which eventually affect big decisions.

At the time, we just kept going. Through trial and error, we had developed a strategy that was working and growing the company.

We continued to progress and did another small financing. Through more trial and error, we got more new customers, and we were on our way.

In 2022, I was seventy-nine. It was time for me to step down. We'd started a search for a new CEO in December 2021. The firm helping us in our search found no good candidates. My son-in-law, Matt, who was president of Mama Mancini's, was not interested in the position. By May 2022, we had not yet found a viable candidate. The search fee was $125,000, with one-third upfront. The firm refunded our deposit, admitting they were having no luck.

We continued the search on our own, using all the contacts we had. In a fairly short time, we had about five candidates that we narrowed down to two. I then hired an outside law firm specializing in contracts. I was set on one particular candidate, Adam Michaels, while half the board that usually voted together as a bloc wanted the other. It was four against three: me, my son-in-law, and another board member who went along with me. We interviewed both candidates and, in the end, I was the only one sticking up for my choice.

After more talking and meeting, we did determine that mine was the best one, and rather reluctantly, the board agreed to hire him.

Michaels turned out to be a good choice. He was young, articulate, and from Mondelez, a major food company. He had a great vision for the company and walked into his new post in September 2022.

At that point, the commodities market began to stabilize. The chicken business was a huge piece of T&L, worth about $25 million per year. When the prices started going down, their margins returned to normal. Then chicken prices hit a record low, just as I became chairman of the board, and then left the company.

Michaels did some good things. He invested in extra personnel for control, operations, and sales. He spent quite a bit more than I did on people, and when he reported to Wall Street, he tended to under-project, while I had over-projected. His way was smart.

On January 31, 2023, I resigned as Chairman of the Board. In June of that year, I sold my interests to a group of hedge fund investors. At that time, the stock was up to $2.80. I netted $2.50, meaning I did very well. My son-in-law sold his shares in December of that year for $3.80. Since then, the stock has continued to go up.

The sale of our stocks created a halo effect because now we had outside investors in the company. And, where we had no analysts following us before the sale of our stocks, we now had four. The trading volume increased from 40,000 a day to 250,000. A lot of people don't want to buy stock without liquidity, which means enough volume in case they want to exit. All of that had the effect of helping Mama Mancini's grow.

The chicken business, particularly at Sam's Club, has skyrocketed. One item in particular quadrupled in volume. Yes, there was a certain amount of luck involved, but good decisions were also made.

Today, Adam Michaels is firmly in control. Margins have increased, and with increased profits, he has invested in people and new equipment. The company is in good hands.

Epilogue

fter I left Mama Mancini's, I took on several consulting jobs, but bowed out by the end of the year.

My big project since then has been this book. While writing it, I haven't only relived the triumphs and failures, but I have also revisited the unique angles from which I approached business challenges.

I think my most interesting failed ventures showed up in product marketing, to the point where today I'm quite happy to own the moniker WACO (Wolf Always Chickens Out).

I tended to take risks in marketing. At one point, I wanted to develop a Mama Mancini's diet. With the help of a nutritionist, I developed a diet centered on items like meatball soup, a frittata, or a vegetable pasta; a full day's calories topping out at 1,400. We had a menu worked out, and I thought it would help us get a lot of publicity while also selling a lot of meatballs.

But my marketing team said, "Look, you have to prove this diet and look at the side-effects, and..."

I chickened out.

Then I had another marketing idea. A friend had a Halloween party where a buddy of his came as Borat, the fictional reporter from Kazakhstan, wearing the T-shirt, boots, and curly wig. They ended up going to the 7-Eleven, where he bought a Slurpee, taking a five-dollar bill out of the front of his pants to pay for it. The clerk wasn't too keen to take the bill.

When I talked to him, he agreed to go to supermarkets, posting on social media about his search for Mama Mancini's meatballs.

My team nixed the idea.

I chickened out.

Then there was the time we hired one of the Real Housewives of New Jersey to be our spokesperson. She wasn't terrific, but after many takes, we completed the commercial, running the ad on Sirius radio. Within hours, we got emails and calls. "How could you put this horrible woman on the radio? I'm never going to buy your meatballs again!"

I think in the end she would have garnered tremendous awareness, but I chickened out.

We made another commercial with someone impersonating Mabel "Madea" Simmons, a character created by Black actor Tyler Perry. In our opinion, it was hysterical. We got one call from a Black person panning it.

I chickened out, and we pulled it.

Interestingly, I have recently had a chance to think about how marketing works today versus early in my career. Today, it is much more fractionalized, making it harder to make an impact. Social media, including Facebook, Instagram, TikTok, YouTube Influencers, and Podcasts, are more important now than TV, radio, magazines, and newspapers. Streaming advertising is a new avenue, but if you have a good product in the right industry, you can gain major market share.

LL: Be aware of the changing environment in social values and the way to communicate through them. Don't get stuck with old concepts.

Looking back, I can see other events in my career as a serial entrepreneur more clearly.

I see how often I listened to bad advice from professional people. But I wonder if that was a crutch, in the sense that over the years, every time I made a bad decision, I blamed it on somebody else. It's a question that needs to be asked because I believe it pays to be honest with yourself.

Another thing I notice is that entrepreneurs tend to be too loyal at times. The rule "Slow to Hire and Fast to Fire" is a good one that I did not always invoke. I made my best decisions in hiring when I slowed the process down and had several meetings and discussions before the new employee joined us. The fast to fire would also apply to the professional advice I got so often.

I became more conservative as I got older and became a better businessman. I learned, as I believe we all do, through adversity. I had challenges, perhaps one at Alpine Lace, and several at Mama Mancini's, but I persevered and marched on. In the end, I made two critical decisions: the hiring of the new CEO, which turned out well, and the acquisition of T&L Salads, as well as a second acquisition of the sales agency that sold us the chicken for T&L.

The chicken acquisition was extremely lucrative for the business. Along with the CEO, I also hired a new accounting team; another good decision.

LL: I learned an ocean full of life lessons, most of which I hope I have passed along here. One big one is the importance of BtoB marketing and understanding what makes people tick. I learned that I seem to be at my best when I am thrown into a crisis, and I know how to find options. It's an invaluable asset.

Now that I have sold all my stock and it has continued to rise, I sometimes ask myself how I feel about that. The fact is, it would have been nicer to have sold it at $8 a share rather than $2.80, but I did well.

I had a good career as an entrepreneur.

I've also had a good life.

As I got older, I also became more honest with myself. Everyone has a veneer, a face they put on. It took going through a major depression for me to become more sensitive to others. But even now, I'll get my sights set on a goal, and forget other people are involved. "Let's do it!" I'll say, without taking into consideration how other people may react.

LL: I learned in later years that if you're the boss and you say something without thinking about it, the person hearing your words can be deeply affected.

You might not compliment someone on a job well done. Perhaps you'll just say, "Thanks for doing the job." Maybe what you should say is, "Thanks. This was a great job."

People take it to heart. They remember, and I didn't realize that until my later years. I would simply go ahead and do what I wanted to do without considering the reaction.

I was just a move-on person. On the flip side, if someone did a job inadequately, I'd tell them. But if it reached the stage where I said nothing, they were eventually gone.

And now, I hope that with this book, I can pay some of my good fortune forward. I hope these Life Lessons will make a difference to other entrepreneurs and aspiring business people. If I can leave you with one thought...

LL: Do what you're good at and do it with honesty, integrity, and determination. Believe in yourself.

Summary of Lessons

Chapter 1:

- If you are confident, life is good. Confidence comes from a desire to be the best, and from the innocence of not realizing life's perils. So, go get 'em, and don't think about it.

Chapter 2:

- Planning and organization are key attributes to business success. How many people do you know who have great skills, but are a mess because they never plan appropriately?
- I think that if you open your horizons and look at unconventional ideas, you'll amaze yourself by what you can create.
- Telling my truth and confronting an unjust issue paid off. I never forgot that. It's not enough to just have strong values. You also have to act on them. You have to stand up for what you believe.
- The day of the pop quiz, I was mortified. I had violated an image I had of myself, and learned an important lesson about how easily your values can falter if you don't guard them and hold yourself up to the standard you've set.

- To the casual observer, we can look perfectly put together and in charge, but do we really know what is going on inside the hearts and minds of the people who look like they have the answer to everything?
- Judging others without basis can be harmful, as my wife always remembered my mother's view of her during our engagement.

Chapter 3:

- I think we are sometimes unfair to our foreign students and foreigners in general. They come from different cultures. Knowing and accepting them can broaden our own outlook on the world and open our minds to new ideas.
- Sometimes adverse conditions come at you unexpectedly, and you just have to deal with them.
- Whenever I read market research polls, or interviews and comments, I carefully peruse the details and statistical analyses, and look at the questions and all their nuances. They can seriously skew the results.

Chapter 4:

- I said nothing when my boss talked to me about how to dress. I instinctively knew that if you tell a long story, it doesn't help you; it only makes it worse. I took my lumps.
- On acquisitions, mergers, or new ventures and ideas, you need a significant supporter.
- I loved playing bridge with my friends on the train going to work. I have no idea if I learned anything from that experience, other than if something brings you joy, go for it!

- There is a god. But, in fact, I was well trained, and the training paid off.
- It's a tired old cliché to say, "Never judge a book by its cover," but old as it is, it's also usually true.
- You may be thrust into strange and even frightening events that you have no control over. Be aware of them and deal with them.
- I learned a valuable lesson during my last year at the Army Reserve camp. Handle what's in front of you, and whatever the situation is, participate. Be there. It works better to make the best of what you've got.

Chapter 5:

- Don't go into business with a relative if you are not in control, and especially, don't go into business with someone who has a different philosophy from yours.
- If you want to do well in business, you have to pay attention, and when things appear to be too good to be true, they are.
- If you're going to cheat, make sure you don't get caught—and you will get caught. Even better? Don't cheat. Not even by a penny.

Chapter 6:

- If you believe in something, stick with it.
- Closed doors only lead to trouble, especially when those meetings happen all day long.
- If you want to be in business, you have to show yourself. It didn't cost a lot to set up that Quonset hut, and it paid off.
- To be successful in BtoB marketing, you have to build personal relationships and make your customers feel important.

- Business relationships that involve making your customer, client, or organization's employees feel wanted, respected, and important are a strong key to success.
- Sometimes, you just have to let it go.
- Go with your instinct.
- The relationship between a mentor and mentee can only survive for so long. Inevitably, the mentee will outgrow the role.

Chapter 7:

- Planning ahead is essential not only to keeping afloat, but also to thriving. And again, the lesson is true that an adverse event can result in a much better outcome.
- In the end, family always wins. I had no doubt we would eventually experience friction as they wanted to exert more control. If we didn't agree on a strategy or issue, they would inevitably call the shots.

Chapter 8:

- You have to plow through it, and you will, even though you don't think you will, you will. You have to go through each day and just get by.
- Sometimes luck really does play a role, or maybe you create your own luck through your instincts.

Chapter 9:

- Don't try to sell a product that isn't good. You have to have a good and sustainable product. If you don't, all the advertising in the world is just hype.
- Be sensitive to others' thoughts and feelings.

- Not everyone is like you. They have different values and ways they operate. However, surprise! They may be a success anyway.
- The way to make an endeavor work is to find a product with virtue, get it into limited distribution, even giving away product, assessing how well it sells, and then making adjustments where needed.
- If you're going to be late, take the time to notify the person.
- It's amazing what we'll do as entrepreneurs to create and sustain our businesses. As an entrepreneur, you have a lot of passion for what you do.
- Don't count your chickens before they've hatched. And also, if it sounds too good to be true, it probably isn't true. I've had to learn that many times.

Chapter 10:

- I'd already learned that people needed to feel they mattered. People get lonely, and it's valuable for them to be in a venue where they can meet their peers.
- We were transparent in all our dealings. Our suppliers and customers appreciated that. They weren't college-educated elites, but they understood the value of hard work, frankness, and honesty.
- The one who has information is king.
- No matter what business you're in, I'd advise you to develop an information set that can be put together quickly in a timely manner, and then use it consistently to evaluate your returns.
- I've found that many times, when you have a problem and you dig in and solve it, you end up with a satisfying result. I tend to do well when I have a problem to deal with.
- "Slow to hire; fast to fire."

Chapter 11:

- If you're at a crossroads in your life, you don't really know what will happen next. The best you can do is move on. I was okay, but I learned that you can't always count on the people you thought you could.
- If you have the gift of being a happy person, it is rare; cherish it.
- Nature can sometimes be in control. Never forget this.
- My wife and I got to meet and know people from all walks of life, and came to understand the value of trust, honesty, and openness. What a valuable lesson!

Chapter 12

- When you bring a group in to help you brainstorm and think, you come up with alternative approaches you may not have thought about. A lot of people could get stuck thinking, "No. This is my idea! My company!" That attitude is not necessarily helpful. You're better off expanding your horizons and being open to new ideas.
- Sometimes, go with luck. Or is it genius? Dudley and his wife made 2,000% on their investment.
- As an entrepreneur, you make a lot of mistakes. The idea is to work your way through them and hopefully learn from them. Most importantly, you need to have people around you who will be honest with you. Probably 70% of entrepreneurs make mistakes. The successful ones are either carried by the marketplace because their idea is that good, or they correct their mistakes. You have to keep that in mind.
- Don't look back. You're not going in that direction.

Chapter 13:

- Listen to your advisor or second-in-command.
- Try unconventional forms of marketing to stand out.
- If you understand what drives middle America, you're a step ahead in marketing your products. In today's world, you have to understand people who use TikTok and other social media platforms.
- Be willing to try new things.

Chapter 14:

- Stop periodically; it's a good idea to pause and take on a learning experience. For me, it was an amazing step forward.
- We were exploring and learning that outside catalysts can really help open your eyes.
- Think outside the box.
- In life, when you start compromising, even little compromises, especially if you compromise your values, you're going to fail.
- You never know if you don't try.
- One of the first lessons I mentioned holds true: people want to feel important.
- The key to success is that the product has to have a natural appeal with sustainable, good-quality virtues, and you have to know how to get it through the distribution channels.
- If you find a business opportunity where your model shows limited risk and great reward, you should really go for it.

Chapter 15:

- If you have a loss, it's better to deal with it right away. When you do that, with the information you have, you're still not guaranteed success, but you're far more likely to be more successful than you would have been otherwise.

Chapter 16:

- Interestingly, both the worst and the best advice can come from professionals. Get a second opinion.
- I tend to do well in the toughest situations, and I think that's because I focus on options. It's helpful to do that. Don't assume any situation is either/or. Look for your options. You may be surprised how many there are. And yes, I was under considerable stress, but sometimes, when you're stretched thin, you do your best work.
- There are always options if you look for them.
- One of our lawyers gave me an excellent piece of advice: Any telephone calls, any communication—only in writing. Everything is on the record. We followed his advice precisely, and it worked.
- "Don't worry about it" means worry about it.
- Deal with an issue up front and look at your options with your partners instead of hiding it.
- Operations is the foundation of your business. Without strong processes and a solid foundation, your business has no value.
- Our marketing plan as an exercise may have been futile, but intellectually and business-wise, I earned several graduate degrees in the process. The lesson is, don't be afraid to go out on a limb and think big.

Chapter 17:

- Stop periodically; it's a good idea to stop and take on a learning experience. For me, it was an amazing step forward.
- Periodically, stopping and taking time for a learning experience is extremely valuable. You just have to open your mind and be willing to make a paradigm shift. It's all information and options.
- You need to be careful with outsiders: they do not always have your best interests in mind.
- Sometimes the best advice is not given with kid gloves. But if you can learn from it, it can be the most valuable.
- If you are in a family business, treat family members with respect and fairness, and do not encourage politicking. It will only lead to major issues later, especially for the employees. This applies to all business relationships.

Chapter 18:

- The product was okay, but the rule is that if it's okay, it's not okay.
- Once again, tread carefully when following legal advice. Watch your every step. Greed can get in the way.
- Avoid lawsuits whenever possible. They can cost more money than they are worth.

Chapter 19:

- Over-projecting profits can cost money.
- The process of gaining information maximized our results and let us know we had done it correctly.
- Don't fall too much in love with yourself.

Chapter 20:

- Don't get waylaid by a moral crusade you're not going to win. Even if you do win, it's not going to do anything for your business.
- Sometimes you have to let people win. Decide what's important and focus on that.

Chapter 21:

- Let a capable partner be noticed and recognized.
- Pay attention to the virtues of the company you are buying and wait until making changes that are carefully thought out.
- When you invest in start-up companies, the risk is much higher, but the reward is also much higher.
- Often, people will have excellent ideas, but when it comes time to implement change, they are too afraid to mess with what they already have, even when change is necessary for growth.
- Possibly, the most important thing I learned is that when you're a consultant or an advisor, many times your advice is not followed, especially if you're advising young people. In fact, many people will ask for advice, but they won't follow it. I didn't learn how to get buy-in until much later.
- The numbers should never lie and should be on time. If you fudge, it makes it worse, and your first loss is your best loss. Believe the numbers.
- When the facts are staring you in the face, it's time to make a hard decision and move on. I liked Mediabay, but they were not realistic about their operations and future.

Chapter 22:

- Today, I believe that after you hit a major milestone, it might be better to just let things settle down before deciding your next step.

Chapter 23:

- If you're going to choose a career path or a business path, you should go into a positive environment that is growing and where the competition is honest. You want to make sure your choice is one where you can make margins and profits, and, if you make mistakes (which you will), the positive aspects of the business will carry you.
- When the going gets rough, slow down and don't panic. We should have lowered our costs until we developed a profitable business.
- Sometimes you forget the life lessons you learn. It may be a good idea every now and then to take stock. I didn't. It's only now, as I'm writing this and looking back, that I see what I did, and how I forgot what I should have known. I think it's better to take stock earlier rather than later.

Chapter 24:

- Our family owned controlling equity in the business, and I should have refused my wife's resignation and lived with the consequences. We lost a valuable asset.
- Some people, when given power, change their modus operandi. You have to be careful not to let that happen to you. If you're involved, you have to be assertive.

- No one likes failure, and when the proverbial s**t hits the fan, blame gets spread around everywhere. When things are good, everyone's happy, but when things go wrong, everyone is unhappy and looking for someone to pin it on.
- You have to pick yourself up. You're going to get hurt at times. Rethink and do what you have to do if you're going to be a successful entrepreneur.
- A steady, consistent strategy and diligence can pay off big. Dig in and don't get discouraged.
- When you know something isn't right, do something about it. We didn't and we paid the price. We were too busy basking in the glory of high sales volumes.

Chapter 25:

- Be careful. If you're going to get involved in a fad, you'd better know what you're doing.
- A good consultant can be a great return on investment.
- Being a good investor in business is very different from being an operator.
- Sometimes you have to grind it out and make a whole lot of small decisions, which eventually affect big decisions.

Epilogue:

- Be aware of the changing environment in social values and the way to communicate through them. Don't get stuck with old concepts.
- I learned an ocean full of life lessons, most of which I hope I have passed along here. One big one is the importance of BtoB marketing and understanding what makes people tick. I learned

that I seem to be at my best when I am thrown into a crisis, and I know how to find options. It's an invaluable asset.

- I learned in later years that if you're the boss and you say something without thinking about it, the person hearing your words can be deeply affected.
- Do what you're good at and do it with honesty, integrity, and determination. Believe in yourself.

Acknowledgements

I wish to thank several people who have inspired me throughout my career:

Ross Lewis, an old friend who suggested I write a book, not on my business successes, but about what I have learned and can teach others.

Marion Wolf, my wife, who is the wisest of all my contacts, and who was a true partner in my career.

Matt Brown, my son-in-law, was a true business partner and very deferential to my experience, but would also gently temper my overexuberance.

Karen Wolf, my daughter, who participated in our family decisions and has an astute understanding of character. She is also a knowledgeable viewer of the current social environment and trends.

Richard Lavin, who was pivotal at times in coaching me in major decisions.

Bill Nash, who is a master salesperson and helped guide me in seeking out new ideas and capital resources.

John Lowry, who has been a friend and major financing resource for the company, even though at times, he was at odds with our goals.

Ken Meyers, a key employee at Alpine Lace and an advisor, and now the principal owner of MCT Dairies.

Vito Catalano, who prepared our Alpine Lace advertising campaign.

Jordan Greenberg, who was our marketing director, presenting key marketing options, and is now president at Splenda.

Noel Ebrahim, who has been a key consultant since 1988 and is now an adjunct professor at the University of South Florida.

Anthony Morello, President of T&L Salads, who, in a short period of time, has proven to be a good friend and an honorable and successful businessperson.

Bob Friedman, who has given me astute legal advice over my career.

Chris DeVito, who has been my personal CPA and advisor.

Steve Greenapple, my personal lawyer and trustee for our family.

Dan Mancini, the inspiration for Mama Mancini's, and a loyal friend.

Priscilla and Jamie Goldman, our marketing support at Mama Mancini's.

Joe Selzer, whose memoir "One Lucky Guy" inspired me to write this book. He is also a very special friend.

Uncle Jerry, the patriarch of our family and my partner in the restaurant business.

Gabe Edelman, sales account executive at Spartan Capital Securities, who strongly supported our Company.

My father, Sam, who inspired me to become an entrepreneur.

Fred D'Agostino, a lifelong friend, key sales agent for Alpine Lace, investor, and Mama Mancini's Board member.

Marty Gross, who was there to invest in my business ventures when needed.

George Wenger, our VP of sales at Alpine Lace, who developed it from start to end.

Bob Davis, a true friend and supporter in many of our businesses.

Barry Siegel, who became a very close advisor and friend until his death.

I want to thank Goody Lindley, who helped edit this book and gave advice on how to present it.

And lastly, thank you to the cop who pulled me over one day. I was driving 46 in a 35 MPH zone. "I'm on my way to a conference call," I explained. "I'm sorry."

"What's the call about?" he asked.

"I'm writing a memoir."

"What's it about?"

"Life lessons from a serial entrepreneur."

His eyes widened. "I'd love to get a copy!"

Nice to know I have at least one reader guaranteed!

About the Author

Carl Wolf can be best described as a self-starting, confident, serial entrepreneur. His life lessons show that success is most often the result of hard work, creativity, and grit.

He was a Phi Beta Kappa Henry Rutgers Scholar in Economics at Rutgers University and graduated as a Beta Gamma Sigma at the top of his class at the University of Pittsburgh, achieving an MBA in marketing. He joined a major NYSE company as an acquisition specialist from 1966-69.

He went on to develop a restaurant chain through Wall Street financing. From there, he helped a subsidiary of a London-based company purchase two acquisitions in the cheese area, as well as developing three specialty cheese businesses. He then moved on to another NYSE company, Standard Brands, followed by consulting work and turning around a major distributor before going into business as an operating consultant in 1978.

He and his wife started a sales agency and cheese-trading business and ultimately founded Alpine Lace in 1981, going public in 1986. Initial investors saw an over ninefold increase in their investment.

After selling Alpine Lace to Land O' Lakes in 1997, he started a software and internet incubator with seven investments and became chairman of the board of a NASDAQ-listed media company. He also purchased a small restaurant as a lark in his hometown and turned it into a major success. He then purchased an appetizer company, which eventually became Mama Mancini's, Inc. (a NASDAQ-listed company), selling his interests to several hedge funds in 2023. Mama Mancini's is now Mama's Creations with a market value of over $350 million.

Today, Carl Wolf lives in North Miami Beach, Florida, and Long Island Beach, New Jersey, with his wife, Marion.

www.ingramcontent.com/pod-product-compliance
Lightning Source LLC
Chambersburg PA
CBHW051525120626
46551CB00012B/1082